ONCE UPON
A PICKET

Muriel Tuttle Eden-Paul

Martin Sisters Publishing

Published by

Martin Sisters Books, a division of Martin Sisters Publishing, LLC

www.martinsisterspublishing.com

Copyright © 2012 by Muriel Tuttle Eden-Paul

ISBN: 978-1-937273-53-8
Cover Art by Abigail Eden
Illustrated by Muriel T. Eden-Paul

Printed in the United States of America
Martin Sisters Publishing, LLC

DEDICATION

To my mother and In memory of my father.

With heartfelt gratitude to the following: to my husband, Michael and our children for believing, to Elizabeth, Greg and Howard for proof-reading; and to my sister, Abigail for her photography. I am thankful toward the following: Gail, Georgia Volunteer Battalion, The Florida Historical Quarterly, and the Citrus County Chronicle; for the use of accounts relating to the soldiers/militia and archeological progress. Much appreciation goes to the Cooper-Pope family for providing my father with a valuable resource; a copy of Major Cooper's personal journal. A special thanks goes to the organization: Friends of Fort Cooper for their devoted dedication and continued support for historical legacy.

In remembrance of Cooper, who spent many devoted days beneath my feet while writing this book.

"It behooves us all—whether landowners or guardians of the public trust – to provide now for the future. For, if those of us who presently have such responsibility do not act wisely and with proper foresight, our children and their children and their children's children shall not know the color of a leaf, or the sound and smells of virgin Florida lake and woodland, or the glorious history which brought such bounty to custody."

~ John H. Eden Jr.

An imprint of Martin Sisters Publishing, LLC

Chapter One

Johnny parked his red truck in front of a sign in the shape of an oak tree with the carved words *A Loving Home for Elders* and azalea bushes planted at its base. A red cardinal greeted him in the alcove as he approached the dark green doors.

Seems like a friendly place, he thought.

The receptionist asked, "May I help you?"

"Yes, ma'am. Mr. Emil, I believe he is in room 7," Johnny replied.

"Yes, Sir. Sign in, please. Turn left. Fourth room on your right."

"Thank you," he replied.

It is hard seeing Mr. Emil in a place like this. At least it smells clean, Johnny thought.

Mr. Emil had moved into the nursing home after his wife, Miss Sadie, died a few years prior. Their only daughter lived in Jacksonville and could not travel to check on him.

Johnny walked down the corridor. As he passed by rooms, televisions flickered and voices whispered. Mr. Emil was a good friend; he was like family. He thought it was ironic, driving his truck to visit Mr. Emil. It used to be the other way around.

When Mr. Emil had come to the farm in his black Model A

pickup truck; a cloud of dust billowed like a giant dust ball rolling down Moccasin Slough. Johnny had watched from his perch in the old, twisted oak. The cloud disappeared when the truck stopped in front of their small red brick house. Mr. Emil stepped out of his truck, chewing on a short stogie and wearing denim overalls and a white T-shirt stained with sweat.

That was then; this is now. Why did it take me so long to visit? How long has it been? Johnny thought. *I had good intentions, but the kids, the grove, the property, the project... The project. Isn't that what brought him here?*

He knocked on the door of Room 7.

"Johnny! Come in!" Mr. Emil sat in his wheelchair, wearing blue denim overalls, a clean white T-shirt, and red-fuzzy slippers. "My daughter sent me these," he said picking up his foot. "They keep my toes warm in this air conditioning. Whatever happened to warm summer breezes and fresh air?"

"It's a hot one today, Mr. Emil," Johnny said. "It feels good in here. Nice place. At least you have a view."

On the bedside table there was a black and white photograph in a thin gold frame. "Look at these three...would ya? I remember that day. You, Pop, and I went to a fish fry my first summer down here. The newspaper guy took it."

"What a string of pan fish! 'Nuf to feed the whole county!" Mr. Emil laughed.

"Maybe back then..." Johnny chuckled. "Not today!"

"This place has really grown! Use to be when you went to town, you knew everybody. Then, more 'n more new faces. Farms and groves bought up, with new houses springin' up all over... 'Specially those subdivisions. It ain't our town anymore." Mr. Emil looked at the photo again, "I shore do miss yo' daddy!"

"So do I. We lost him too soon," Johnny agreed.

"Quiet man, hard worker. Never knew a feller so driven to leave the city and become a citrus farmer. He fit right in, though. Everybody liked him. He was always recitin' limericks. He loved

8

limericks!"

Johnny smiled.

"He sure took an interest in the history of this area. He taught you well," Mr. Emil continued.

"You both did," Johnny said.

"Settlers started homesteadin' the territory, and then the Seminoles moved into this area to find refuge in the Cove." Mr. Emil retold the history Johnny had heard so often. "Then things started gettin' pretty bad--not enough room for everybody."

"I think I know how they feel," Johnny said. "Not enough elbow room now. People spreading out and getting too close."

"Well, you know what they say. 'That's progress!'" Mr. Emil chuckled.

"I guess so. There's progress being made about the fort site."

"Whatcha mean?" Mr. Emil looked shocked. "Ya don't mean yore sellin' out after all these years and developin' the property?"

"What?" Johnny was surprised that Mr. Emil would even suggest such a thing. "Of course not. I have had well-meaning friends tell me I should, or keep it for myself and build a house there. I just couldn't. The letters and research I mailed to the state have generated a lot of interest. Here, I brought you some responses from Tallahassee. This one is dated July sixth, 1970, from the Attorney General's office."

"Well, I'll be. Read 'em to me."

"Yes, sir. 'The old fort is indeed one of our state's historic landmarks, and I will be interested in the report now being prepared by the Division of Recreation and Parks... ' Another one from Commissioner Doyle Connor, July seventh, 1970: 'It is apparent you have done an awful lot of historical research, and I compliment you on your willingness to put in that much time and effort in order to tell the story about your section of the state of Florida.' Here's one from Governor Kirk, July fourteenth, 1970. 'Florida needs to preserve its historical sites, many of which are too rapidly disappearing. Your efforts are greatly appreciated.' Another one

9

from Attorney General Faircloth, dated August fourteenth, 1970 says, 'I agree with you that our state is endowed with a treasure of natural resources. Projects such as the one you now propose are of great help in preserving the beauties of the State of Florida. Thank you for the interest and responsibility you have shown in helping to preserve a little bit of Florida for our children and their children. With warmest personal regards, I am, sincerely, Earl.'"

When Johnny finished reading excerpts from the letters sharing Tallahassee's support, Mr. Emil exclaimed, "You're kiddin' me! This is wonderful news. That kind of progress, I like hearin' about!"

"There's more. There's going to be some rumblin' through our woods," Johnny smiled. "Tallahassee is sending a team of archeologists down."

"You're kiddin'."

"No," Johnny laughed. "They're coming in a few weeks. After all the years of research and letter-writing, someone's finally taking an interest in the possibility."

"Possibility? It's not a possibility; it's not maybe... It's there, and it's real!" Mr. Emil stated. "They'll see."

"Well, I'm tiring you out," Johnny said. "Betty's expecting me home for supper."

"How are Betty and the kids?" Mr. Emil asked.

"Betty sends her love, and the kids are fine. Little brown berries running barefoot all summer and swimming. School starts in a couple of weeks."

Mr. Emil whispered, "Don't be a stranger, Partner! Next time you come, can you bring me some fried chicken and biscuits? The food here tastes nothin' like Miss Sadie's cookin'. And maybe a ceegar?"

Johnny took Mr. Emil's frail hand in his and shook it. The older man did not have the same grip he once had. It wasn't the broad, giant hand, leathered from hard work and sun, which once tousled his uncombed, summer-blond, hair. Johnny gave Mr. Emil's hand a firm shake. He paused and looked deep into the old man's eyes, where tears swelled in pockets of loose skin.

Johnny's eyes stung as he whispered, patting their clasped fingers with his other hand, "I'll see what I can do. Goodbye."

He made a point to say that word: "Goodbye." It was a difficult word for him to speak, as it had been since he was ten years old; sitting on a northbound train at the end of his first summer. He had watched Pop waving from the platform with the word "goodbye" stuck somewhere between his stomach and his throat.

"Goodbye, Mr. Emil." He waved at the door.

"Goodbye, son."

Later, Johnny walked into their kitchen and his wife, Betty, kissed him hello.

"How's Mr. Emil?" she asked.

"He's okay. It's hard to see him in a place like that."

"I heard Live Oak is pretty nice," she responded sweetly.

"It is, but I don't want to end up like that. It was hard to lose Pop so quickly, but maybe it was better... I mean for him to have gone so soon." He cleared his throat. "Anyway, Mr. Emil asked about you and the kids. He was hopin' you'd make him some fried chicken and biscuits."

"I'd love too. I consider that a compliment 'cause Miss Sadie was a real good cook." Betty smiled, "Wash up for supper and call the kids.

After dinner, Johnny walked toward the small red barn, wondering how many steps he had covered over the years back and forth. He had followed Pop to the barn to milk their Jersey cows for a dairy route, which helped get their grove started. The stalls had emptied over the years, and his yellow Caterpillar bulldozer was parked in front of them.

Johnny started the engine with a loud rumble, and then backed the huge machine off the wood boards, and parked it in the shade. He checked the hydraulic ram, raised and lowered the front blade, and oiled all moving parts.

"We have an important job to do and you're going to look your best," he said, as if the yellow 'dozer could hear him.

The next morning he drove the bulldozer through the Bahia pasture and timber of long-leaf pine trees until he reached the other side of his farm. He crossed the road and drove through thick palmetto, oaks, and wild magnolia draped in vines. The loud, yellow monster muted sounds of katydids, tree frogs, and birds beneath the hammock until he stopped on the bluff. The bulldozer had invaded the woods like an alien spaceship.

It was by most calendars autumn, but Florida did not adhere to the seasonal schedule of northern states. Autumn still felt like summer. It was hot and muggy, and the bugs were plentiful. The only certainty that summer was over was their children were back in school, except the youngest daughter, Abby.

"They're here, Daddy!" she yelled from her perch in the old, twisted oak tree, where she had climbed to get a better look.

The caravan of state vehicles drove down their lane lined with water oaks. Junko barked his deepest woof to see and hear so many cars all at once.

"Good boy. It's okay, I've been expecting them." Johnny patted his Rottweiler, and the solid muscled dog leaned into him. "It's okay. Sit." Junko wagged his short, stubby tail, and then sat by his side.

Johnny waved to the first car, giving the driver the all clear. A gentleman stepped out, wearing khaki pants and shirt, a pith helmet, short trimmed beard and held a curved pipe between his teeth.

"You must be Professor Frank?" Johnny greeted him and shook his hand.

"Yes, sir. Johnny, it's a pleasure to meet you. I just returned from a dig in Egypt. I wasn't sure if I would make this assignment."

"Well, we aren't as old as Egypt around here," Johnny chuckled. "But I think you'll find it interesting."

Junko interrupted the two men. He had waited long enough to be introduced and decided to do the formality himself. He leaped up and put both paws on the professor's chest.

"Whoa! And who is this fellow?"

"Down," Johnny scolded. "This is Junko. I'm sorry; it's my fault. I should've introduced him first."

The men laughed while Junko sat and waited for his greeting from the professor.

"Hi ya, boy," Professor Frank patted the dog. "Do you shake?" Junko held up his paw.

"We'll be seeing a lot of each other." He smiled, biting his pipe stem.

As far as Junko was concerned, all was well, so he ran up to each vehicle to say hello. The passengers stood near their vehicles and he gave them a good sniff. His body swayed from side to side with each pat on the head and "Hi ya' boy!"

Betty walked outside helping Abby out of the tree, and the two of them joined the men. Johnny introduced them to the professor.

"This is my wife, Betty, and youngest daughter, Abby."

Betty and Abby shook the professor's hand.

"Welcome," said Betty. "It's such a pleasure to meet you."

"How do you do?" Abby said, proud she remembered Mama's final instructions.

"Nice to meet you both. Now's a good time for ya'll to meet the team." Professor Frank walked down the line of people and made introductions.

After handshakes and "Nice to meet ya'lls", Professor Frank was eager to move on. "Are we ready to head for the site?"

"If anybody needs to freshen up they are welcome," Betty offered.

"That might not be a bad idea, thank you. Here, Johnny, take one of these." The Professor handed him a walkie-talkie. "We can talk to each other, we all have one."

Soon everyone had gotten back into their vehicles, and Johnny's red pickup was in the lead. Betty sat at his side, while Junko and Abby rode in the bed of the truck. Abby's legs dangled over the edge of the tailgate, while her arms wrapped securely around

Junko's big chest.

"Move 'em out," Johnny called, "Over and out."

While Johnny's truck idled at the gate of the pasture, he spoke into the walkie-talkie. "Betty will open the gate. Have your rear van close it after they're through. Got some cattle grazing in here."

"Roger!" Professor Frank responded and radioed to the rear van with the instructions.

Betty, dressed in blue jeans, a soft floral print blouse, and navy-blue canvas sneakers, slipped the chain off the post and pushed the gate out of the way. Johnny passed through the gate and stopped so she could climb back into the cab. Her green eyes sparkled with yellow specks. Short brunette curls adorned her head, framing her slim facial features and high cheekbones.

He winked at her, "You look beautiful."

She slid back to her seat next to him and kissed his cheek.

"We've been waiting a long time for this day," he whispered. "Thank you for everything, darlin'."

"Yes, we have," she smiled. "I can hardly believe the dig is going to happen."

Abby tapped on the window. "Hurry up. You're goin' to let the cows out!"

She knew too well what would happen if the gate was left open too long. A weekly event, it seemed--someone would leave the gate open, and they would have to chase the cows back into the pasture.

"Okay honey," Johnny waved.

The Black Angus and Brahman cattle looked up from grazing to see traffic in their pasture. Some white egrets took flight off the cows' backs at the commotion, but others stayed to eat bugs.

Abby sang the silly song she and her sisters made up. "Cow-bird ridin' high, Rustlin' up some grub. There's more, there's more so join the club. Cow-bird, Cow-bird, eating a buggy snack, standing upon Brahma's hump-back."

Abby was glad she didn't have to go to kindergarten, but she missed her brother and sisters riding with her in the pick-up through the field. The grass pinged beneath the truck in rhythm to her song. The pinging stopped when the truck came to a halt. Once they reached the other side, they came upon another gate, which Betty opened.

"The property's across the road. I'll cross the Ol' Flora City Road, pull ahead, and wait." Johnny radioed to the Professor. "Have your rear car close the gate and radio me once he has crossed over."

"Roger!"

After they crossed over, they traveled a dirt road slowly, through a thicket of palmettos with long, slender leaves shaped like fans. Small sticks and branches scratched the sides of the vehicles, snapping against the metal. They drove through the hammock to a clearing and stopped at the shore of the beautiful, pristine, spring-fed Lake Holathlikaha.

"I never expected to see this!" Professor Frank exclaimed.

"Instant cool," Jamie, a college student shouted.

"Yeah, man. We'll take this kind of dig any day," said Mike.

"Is this where the dig is?" Jamie asked.

"No, the dig will begin on the bluff." Johnny pointed, and everyone turned to look.

On the northwest side of the lake, surrounded by a wall of trees, shrubs, and grasses, a natural opening exposed a bluff.

"Over there," Johnny pointed. "That's where we'll dig. We'll have to walk everything over."

Professor Frank scanned the site to see where to set up their equipment. He saw the bluff, lake, trees, and…a bright yellow bulldozer parked under the shade of the oaks.

"Excuse me, Johnny, but what is *that* doing here?"

Johnny spoke with confidence. "It's mine. I'm going to clear away more than a hundred years for you."

Professor Frank dropped the pipe from his lips and stared at Johnny in surprise. He cleared his throat, picked up his pipe and wiped the sand off on his pants. He put the pipe back in his mouth, chewed on the tip and did not say a word. He looked toward the water, the bluff, again at the bulldozer, and then at Johnny.

"I appreciate it, but…well, a bulldozer isn't exactly an archeologist tool," the professor said, thoughtful of Johnny's feelings. "Searching for artifacts is delicate work. I…"

"I realize that, but I can save you a lot of time. There are only a few people who understand what lies beneath our feet: Betty, Mr. Emil, and me. I wouldn't do anything to hinder finding it," Johnny declared.

The professor took off his helmet and scratched his head, then readjusted his hat. The rest of the team waited to receive their instructions. Everyone wondered with anticipation if the bulldozer's engine would start up.

"I don't understand what I am about to say, but I am going to say it… Johnny start your engine!"

"You won't be disappointed," Johnny assured him as he climbed into the seat. He took a bottle of cola out of the blue cooler, and a cigar out of his top pocket. Once he started the engine a puff of black smoke dissipated into the trees. Professor Frank yelled above the roar of the engine. "Okay everybody start unpacking and set up your stations!" For nearly two weeks, Johnny worked the control levers back and forth with precision. The curved blade peeled layers of debris and topsoil out of the way. Even though the bulldozer was a heavy machine, it seemed to glide across the sandy earth as if the tracks never touched the ground. He carefully removed layers of soil down to the root level in long strips in the area he believed was where the picket once stood. After he finished, Johnny parked the bulldozer beneath the shade of an oak tree and turned off the engine.

He climbed out of the seat and yelled, "She's all yours Professor!"

"Listen up, people. We'll start working in this area," Professor Frank indicated with an arc of his arm. "Rita and Robin, take the screens over there." He pointed. "Mike set up the survey camera on the bluff. If you haven't done so, spray yourselves with repellant. The bugs are in full force this morning!" He slapped a horsefly against his neck. "Boy, these things don't give up, do they? Johnny, we're going to trowel the trenches."

With great anticipation, everyone began his or her work in hopes of revealing a part of history. Professor Frank and Johnny dug the trenches in the stifling heat. They cleaned the deep strips, gently scraping with trowels and sweeping lose sand with whiskbrooms.

"I'm hot and thirsty, Mama," Abby complained.

"Get a drink from the cooler," Mama suggested.

Abby skipped over to see what Jamie was doing. The college student wore a bandanna tied around his head to catch the sweat, before it dripped into eyes. Shirtless, he wore frayed jean shorts and canvas sneakers full of holes.

"Whatcha doing?" Abby yelled to him.

He wore earphones, listening for bleeps; he swept the flat disc back and forth over the sand in the bulldozer cuts. He did not hear her.

She tapped him on the back. "Whatcha doin'?" Abby yelled to him again, louder than before.

He stopped his work. "I'm listening for bleeps which tell me if metal is beneath the surface," Jamie answered.

"Can I try?" She asked.

He put the earphones over her ears. "I'll scan. You listen."

"I don't hear anything," she complained. "How come your toes are stickin' out of your sneakers?"

"It's cooler that way." He smiled. "You can stay and watch, but you have to be quiet so I can hear the bleeps."

"Okay," she said, but she soon tired of his work and walked back to her mother. "Find anythin'?"

"Not yet. Abby, we have to be patient if we're going to find any artifacts," Mama told her.

"What's a 'tifac?"

"Well, it's something very old which was left behind by people in the past and can tell us a little about them," Mama explained.

For about two weeks, they trowelled the surface of the trenches and scanned the metal detectors back and forth over the whole area. Finally on the first day of the third week, Jamie heard, *bleep*... He swiped again...*bleep*.

"Professor, I think we found something!" He shouted.

Professor Frank trowelled the area where the bleeps were the loudest. "You sure did!"

The professor picked up a jacket-size button.

"There's another bleep, sir."

This time the trowel clinked against a tin-drinking cup, darkened by time. Johnny and Professor Frank examined the found artifacts. "They're definitely appropriate for the period," the professor confirmed.

Everyone came over to examine the button and cup.

"Look, Abby, a drinking cup. Just think; a militia man or soldier could've drunk some water from the spring out of this cup," Johnny explained to his wide-eyed daughter.

"Can I do it too? Can I drink from this too?" she begged.

"Not with this one," he smiled.

Professor Frank and Johnny worked side by side in the trenches. They scraped and swept each square inch with tedious care and determination. The following day, the whiskbroom swept across and brushed away fine granules of sand to reveal a dark circle.

"It's a post mold!" Professor Frank exclaimed.

"I'll be. We found it. Betty! Betty!" Johnny shouted. "We found it!"

Betty ran over to the trench with the rest of the team behind her. They peered over the edge of the trench and saw the post mold.

"Our first indication," Professor Frank pointed. "The pine logs used for a picket disintegrated leaving discolored soil. It's a ghostly reminder of the past. Johnny, there's got to be more. We'll keep working in line."

The archeology students joined them in the trenches with trowels and whiskbrooms in hand. There was not a breath of air moving under the trees laden with vine and moss. No one noticed the heat anymore. It did not seem to matter; the only thing that mattered was to uncover the past, which they did with every post mold revealed. First, they found the south wall of the fort, west of where the tin cup and jacket button were unearthed. By the end of the week they had exposed the south, west, and north walls and a partial section of the east wall. They were then able to map the actual location where the picket once stood. It was, indeed, Fort Cooper.

*"I don't understand what I am about to say, but I am going to say it
... Johnny, start your engine!"*

Chapter Two

By November of 1971, the east wall had also been excavated. They had discovered a gap in the east wall facing the lake about twenty-five feet, possibly to have access to the fresh water spring, which gurgled beneath the glistening lake. Johnny and Professor Frank finished mapping out the uncovered post molds and post remains.

"Now that this phase is complete, we need to call an informal press conference," Professor Frank announced.

Johnny notified the newspapers around the state. The journalists arrived with their leather bags filled with tape recorders, pencils, pads, and cameras. The reporters, along with some members of the Citrus County Historical Society, toured the grounds.

"I drank from this spring like soldiers, Seminoles, and homesteaders had done before me. Ever since I was a boy, I heard the stories of the old timers that a fort did exist near this spring," Johnny pointed toward Lake Holathlikaha. "April second, 1836, Major Cooper, commanded five companies of the First Georgia Battalion of 380 volunteers. They followed orders to build a fortification on this bluff," he continued. "Major Cooper did indeed build the picket, which sustained him and his men while they held their position and waited for the relief troops. The relief troops returned much later than anticipated on April eighteenth, 1836." Johnny pointed to the ghostly remains of the past, which were once fort walls.

Professor Frank said, "We're now open for questions."

One reporter asked, "How's it possible that so much detailed excavation has been accomplished within such limited time?"

Professor Frank laughed and looked at Johnny. "Johnny pushed these mounds of earth with his bright yellow Caterpillar."

There was a murmur in the crowd.

"First of all, we didn't have to hunt long for the fort itself because of Johnny's research on the oral history of Citrus County. His investigation of Georgia's history and Major Cooper's volunteer battalion of foot soldiers. It put us right on target. Secondly, we never could have done it without that bulldozer," he laughed. "Johnny handled that machine as delicately as I do my trowel, and a bulldozer isn't exactly what one would call an archeological tool."

The crowd chuckled.

Another reporter looked around at the scenery, "Johnny, how did you know where to look? What made you pinpoint this exact spot in over seven hundred acres?"

"As I mentioned earlier, the oral history of this area was embedded in me at an early age. I wanted to learn more and began questioning long-time residents of the county--what stories they had heard from their great-grand father that, by chance, would indicate what happened here. In every instance, they took me to the same spot: a bluff on the west side of the lake where an ancient oak tree stood near the water's edge. They would point and say this is where the fort was," Johnny recalled.

After most of the group had gone, a few reporters remained. "It was in the silence of the late afternoon," one reporter later wrote, "that we began to fully realize this windfall that has come to us. For a few moments we looked out over the lake. What a sight it must have been well over a hundred years ago as those near-helpless volunteer soldiers viewed the same scene. And here, too, could have well stood Osceola, the Great War chief of the Seminoles, when once the fort was abandoned after the two weeks siege."

MURIEL TUTTLE EDEN-PAUL

.

.

Chapter Three

The year was 1931; ten-year-old Johnny looked out his window over the garden and yawned. Winter held fast to New England's spring morning.

"Another 'not yet' day," he whispered, waking up for school.

Spring had teased Johnny with moments of warmth, purple crocus, and sounds of water dripping off the roof. Spring had smelled briefly like damp earth, wormy and moist. Spring promised summer when the robins returned, but then winter would say, "Not yet!" and took spring away, like it did that morning.

Johnny dressed in his scratchy wool suit mother had set out for him. He wet his tousled blond hair and tried to comb the cowlick down. As he walked to the back stairs that led to the kitchen, he passed small servant rooms off the long hallway. The rooms were empty except for Mrs. Jaeger, who lived in the room at the top of the stairs. The wood-planked floors were painted brown with a braided oval rug placed by her iron bed; neatly made with a striped blue and cream wool blanket. A small window overlooked the garden. The light from the window haloed a yellowed photograph of her husband, dressed in a uniform. After Mrs. Jaeger lost her husband and the rest of her family in WWI, she had immigrated to New York

City. She answered Pop's advertisement for a cook, and he hired her on the spot. Johnny had known her his whole life.

His footsteps echoed on the polished wooden steps all the way down to the kitchen. The kitchen seemed bright and cheerful, even on such a gloomy, grey day. The polished black and white tile floor glistened in the light. Mother's collection of dishes added bright color through glass-paned cabinets. The smell of robust coffee and burnt toast met his nose. He knew Mother waited for him in the dining room.

Lizzy Jaeger looked up from the pot she was stirring and greeted him in German. "Gut morgen Meister John!"

"How can you be so cheerful? Did you look outside?" Johnny scowled.

She wiped her hands on her apron and hugged him. His cheek pressed against her green uniform made from oiled calico. She smelled of bacon and Lily of the Valley.

"Your mother is waiting for you in the dining room. I'll bring your breakfast."

"Good morning, Johnny!" Mother sipped her black coffee from a dainty porcelain cup and took a bite of burnt toast. "Try some; it's good for digestion."

"Good morning, Mother," he kissed her cheek and sat next to her. "No, thank you."

Mrs. Jaeger, set his bowl of oatmeal in front of him with a pitcher of fresh cream, a bowl of sugar, cinnamon, butter, and three slices of bacon. She smiled, "*Heiß Hafermehl ohne Klumpen!*"

Johnny laughed. She had made his oatmeal just the way he liked it: "hot with no lumps." His first bite of creamy-sweet, buttery-cinnamon oatmeal went down smooth and warmed him on the inside.

"Anything else, Ma'am?" Mrs. Jaeger asked.

"No, we're fine, thank you."

After breakfast, Johnny's mother wrapped his woolen scarf around his neck and kissed him on the cheek.

"Mother, it itches. Do I have to wear it?" he complained.

"It will keep the cold out of your chest, and your heart will stay warm for me." She smiled and kissed him again, on the other cheek. "Study hard, dear."

In the classroom, Johnny sat in a hard oak chair and stared at the wall clock. Today was Friday, which meant Grandfather and Grandmother would come for dinner, two days with no school, and hopefully, a postcard from Pop. Sometimes, Pop took him on business trips, but this trip to Florida he had gone alone. He had been gone longer than Johnny expected.

Pop had taken him to Europe once; they visited old castles, which stood untouched for centuries. They had gone to museums and world fairs. Johnny learned history from the places he visited rather than the classroom. He liked hearing stories. Mrs. Jaeger told him about the old country. Grandfather told him stories about Florida when the railroad came through. Pop's stories were about the Seminole Indians living in Florida's swamps.

His mind was not on math. A black crow called his attention out the window. It flapped its wings trying to balance on a flimsy maple branch. Meanwhile the rest of the class recited multiplication tables. Rough woolen knickers and stockings scratched his legs. His collar was buttoned too tight and with his black tie choked him. The rattle of reciting voices faded in his daydream about a warmer place-- Florida, where Pop was. It was a place where he could take off his tie, woolen knickers, and stockings. It was a place where he could run barefoot if he wanted to. Florida would be summer all year round. No more cold winter and no more cold spring.

Study hard, dear. He remembered his mother's words, as he watched the crow outside. Then it began to snow. Morning's winter promise had been delivered. Huge, white, wet, fluffy flakes fell against dark skeleton trees, which surrounded the school and village.

Whack.

The head master quickly rapped his ruler across the back of Johnny's hand. The class had picked up their graphite and were practicing their handwriting. Johnny had been caught daydreaming again. His hand stung, but he picked up his graphite and joined his classmates. He squeezed his eyes to stop any wetness, which had begun to swell in them. He did not to look up from his work. The only sound was graphite sliding across papers of fifteen young boys in the fourth grade at Middleton Academy. The points tapped softly against the wooden desks. It seemed an eternity until the bell rang and class was dismissed. Little men of all ages walked down the hall in an orderly fashion. As soon as the huge oak doors flung open, a bedlam of boys filled the courtyard flailing snowballs at one another. Cries and yells echoed in the village as their snowball fight ensued and delayed Johnny's arrival home.

"I'm home!"

No one answered. His coat dripped on the tapestry rug in the front hall.

"Mother? Mrs. Jaeger? Anybody here?"

On the entry table laid a postcard postmarked from Florida with a green one-cent stamp. He picked it up with his wet, cold fingers and read aloud.

Dear Son,

I saw an alligator sunning itself on our bank yesterday. He must have been 10 feet! I miss you. Give Mother a kiss.

Pop

He turned over the postcard. A picture of green alligators with menacing grins encircled their twenty-nine babies, with the words *Alligators, natives of Florida.* His hands felt warm as he held it. He ran to his room and put it next to the others--the old Tampa Bay Hotel, palm trees, cypress knees, and a steamboat.

"*Hellooooo.* Anybody home? Mother? Mrs. Jaeger?" Johnny yelled.

"In the kitchen, Johnny," Mrs. Jaeger answered back.

He ran into the kitchen. "Did you see the alligators Pop sent?"

"Did he now?" She laughed. "I'm glad it is too cold in New England for the likes of them."

28

"Well, just think; they are sunning their scaly backs in the warm sunshine. We're freezing, and it's snowing outside," Johnny said.

"Yes, you have a point there," she smiled. "But I think I will take my chances with a snowball. Would you like some cookies and hot tea?"

"Yes, please," Johnny said. "What's for dinner? I'm starving." A kettle hissed on the stove as Mrs. Jaeger rolled out yeast dough for rolls. "Roast lamb and mashed potatoes. I have an idea. Why don't you take some cookies and hot tea out to your mother. She's in her studio."

Mrs. Jaeger prepared a basket of gingersnaps and Earl Grey tea.

Johnny said, "When we visited Florida, I saw an alligator once. I saw three bumps floating on top of the water--two eyes, and a nose."

"Better you than me," she teased. "Here, let me get the door for you."

"Thank you," Johnny said, as he walked outside with his basket.

He looked up at the grey sky as snowflakes fell on his face. He followed the snow-covered path spattered with rabbit tracks until they disappeared beneath the boxwood hedge where small sparrows hid. Smoke curled out of the stovepipe from the studio's stove, carrying the smell of warmth from burning wood. He peeked in the window at Mother, who wore her indigo frock and grey jacket. Her hair was pinned back out of her eyes with a few brown strands falling on her forehead. She had modeled clay into a male figure, a railroad worker, who held a pick ax and a lantern. Her fingers pressed into the clay making small folds in his overalls. Mother startled as the door opened.

"Oh, Johnny! I was deep in thought and didn't hear you. Come in, come in." She waved her hand, still holding a chunk of wet clay.

"Is he done, Mother?" Johnny asked.

"Almost," she sighed, "but as luck would have it, the Depression hasn't favored the arts, among other things. Perhaps the exhibition will have to wait."

When she saw the basket, she said, "Oh, how lovely. Tea. Bless you," and lifted the napkin to peek. "And cookies. What a lucky Mother I am."

She kissed him on the cheek and wiped her hands on her jacket stained with clay and paint. She poured the teapot, filling the two cups.

"Here sit by the fire and tell me about your day." She wrapped her cold hands around the warm cup.

"Boring. It was nothing," Johnny said.

"I don't like that word, boring. You're not allowed to say it. There's no excuse in this life to be bored. We can always find something to do with the talents God blesses us with," Mother scolded.

They each took a bite of a gingersnap cookie.

"Mmmm, perfect 'snap', Mrs. Jaeger put in just the right amount of pepper. Oh, I didn't realize how hungry I was."

"If I was with Pop, I wouldn't be bored," Johnny reminded her. "Why is he still gone? Shouldn't he be home by now?"

"His business took him longer than expected," Mother looked outside and quickly changed the subject. "Blue skies, Johnny," she announced. "I'm finished for the day. We need to get ready for Grandmother and Grandfather." She had received a letter from her husband, John. He had written that a small brick home and pole barn had been built. He was ready to leave the north to make a new life for his family. She wrote him back saying that she was staying in New England. This, however, was not something she could share with her son. Not now.

Johnny was glad his grandparents were coming over. They had returned on the train from Florida a few days before, and he had not seen them yet. Johnny and Mother did not go down with them this year. Johnny hoped they would have news of Pop and more Florida stories to tell.

They walked back toward the garden and the sun had melted the snow in his old tracks. He reached down and packed wet snow together, grinning.

Whack. He hit his mother square in the back.

"Oh, so that's how it's going to be?" Mother said, pretending to be angry. "Here try this!"

Wham. She hit him in the shoulder.

"You throw like a girl!" Johnny laughed. He threw another snowball but missed.

"You missed." Mother threw again. Her aim was good--a direct hit. "Do you mean you wish YOU threw like a girl?"

They laughed and hollered as they pelted each other with snowballs until they reached the back door.

Mother said excitedly, "Oh, Look! Spring *is* just around the corner!"

A cluster of purple and yellow crocus buds wearing snowcaps on their pointy heads reached for the sun. Johnny stopped to look at them. *What's Pop doing right now?* He wondered.

*

As crocus pushed up through warmed earth in New England, John cleared his field of the last palmetto and scrub pine, in rural North Central Florida, until he had enough to burn. He wiped the sweat off of his brow and looked toward the sun.

If this was hot for spring, what will summer be like? He wondered.

Every winter since the late 1880s, his wife's family had been coming to Florida. His father-in-law bought acreage for his phosphate business and as an investment. Many northerners bought land in the south with big dreams for this tropical paradise. Some came to grow citrus, plant crops, or build hotels for winter retreats. All of them sought a lifestyle the climate offered. John had joined his father-in-law's investment company, as well as their winters in Florida.

John made a deal with his father-in-law to take some acreage in scrub pine and palmettos on the shores of a small lake. He had built a small, red-brick two-bedroom house and a pole barn with a tin roof for his Jersey cows. Once the house was ready, he left New England in the fall with hopes his family would soon join him. However, he had not expected his wife's reluctance to leave New England, especially, since Florida had been a second home to her. She had, however, agreed to let Johnny stay with him over the summer.

He lit a match to the brush pile. "When Johnny comes this summer, we'll start planting this field with rows of seedlings," he said to himself.

The Depression had hit the peninsula far sooner than the rest of the country. People were giving up and moving on. John was able to find what he needed to start his grove and farm at a cheap price. During the Depression years, Florida's mild winters invited many people to come to the state looking for work in the turpentine distilleries, truck farming, or fishing along the coast. If they could not prove they had jobs, they were stopped at the state line. Fortunately, John had land and a job. He was there to stay.

After his evening meal of cornbread and bacon he sat on his porch and watched an old gator float by in the still water.

"Right on time, ol' fellow," John whispered, "I can't wait for Johnny to see you!"

The night sky cast a lavender hue over the water.

"You be still, Oscee." The mutt growled.

"Let him pass without a fuss," John said to his new friend. "Okay?"

Oscee looked up at his new master, gave a sigh, and laid his head across John's dusty boots.

"I wonder how Johnny liked the picture of the gators I mailed him?"

Oscee wagged his tail gently against the floorboards.

"I'm sure glad you wandered to my place, pup," John said as he stroked the dog's head. "It feels like you and I have always been here."

The two of them sat in silence until bullfrogs interrupted the quiet with bass and cello voices, which bounced off lily pads.

"Goodnight boy," John walked back inside the darkened house as the screen door slammed behind him.

He turned on the gas lamp and washed in the basin. Before turning in, he picked up another post card with a portrait of Osceola, a leader of the Seminole Indians, with his son after a hunt. John wrote with a broken yellow pencil.

Dear Johnny, Look at the rabbit Osceola's son is holding. The boy looks just about your age. A long time ago they lived in the Cove of the Withlacoochee. Osceola walked on our farm! I Miss you, Pop

John was tired after his hard work in the field and chores around the farm. It was late for him, but not for his son, whose evening in New England had only begun.

Chapter Four

Grandfather banged the brass doorknocker, the sound echoed through the house. Johnny ran downstairs and leaped over the last few steps, landing with a loud thud.

Punctual, as always, he thought and opened the door to greet his grandparents.

"Butler John," Grandfather teased, "is your mother at home?"

"Here, let me take your coats," Johnny said politely. "Mother's in the kitchen with Mrs. Jaeger. I got a postcard from Pop today!" He had taken the post card down to show his grandparents and reached into his jacket pocket. "How was your train trip?"

"Long and tiring," Grandmother fanned herself.

"Well, we can't complain dear. At least we weren't covered in soot like the good old days," Grandfather chuckled.

"Here, let me put on my spectacles." Holding the postcard at arm's length, he read, "Aha, alligators! 'Florida Native.' I guess they are the true natives of the state. *Ah.* There's my darling daughter, Margaret. So good to see you."

"Mother, you look so lovely. Father, always the dapper gentleman," Johnny's mother said, kissing their cheeks.

Grandmother's gray hair was piled loosely on top of her head in a bun. Her slim waist was wrapped in a lace belt, which matched the cape collar across her narrow shoulders.

"Mother, you've had this outfit for nearly twenty years," Johnny's mother declared. "And you still look stunning in it."

"Yes," Grandfather said, "she looks just as lovely as she did thirty years ago."

Grandmother blushed at his compliment. "My dear, why should I get rid of a perfectly good outfit? I am much too old to wear the frocks you young women wear today." She turned to her grandson, "Besides, I think it goes well with my mourning brooch, don't you?" Your great-grandmother's epitaph pinned to my collar," she patted it.

Johnny nodded politely, even though he thought Grandmother's mourning brooch just a little eerie. Her brooch was a small glass oval with great-grandmother's hair woven into a tiny flower and a little pearl at its center. Once it was popular for people to save hair from a loved one. Johnny remembered Grandmother's story about a lady who saved hair from her children and other family members wiped out by influenza. She wove their hair into individual hair-flowers, each one a different shade of hair color: black, brunet, red, blond, or grey. Then she arranged the hair flowers into an elaborate still life and framed it in gold.

"Father, can I get you a sherry?"

"Maragret! This is Prohibition. Are you buying on the black market?" Her father teased, "What would the Temperance Ladies think?"

Grandmother smiled. She knew her modern daughter would not worry about what they thought.

Mrs. Jaeger rang the dinner bell, and Johnny led the way into the dining room, which looked beautiful. Mother chose her Irish linen tablecloth and china dishes with the colorful floral sprigs, a sprinkling of dots, and a gold trim in the center of each plate. In the middle of the table, a crystal vase was filled with narcissi and asparagus fern. Even though there were only four of them, the table had been set for five. Mother insisted on setting an extra place just in case there might be an unexpected visitor. Sometimes someone did, like Uncle Charles, Reverend Thomas, or Widow Ida. The extra plate gave Johnny comfort Pop would come back soon.

"Your table looks beautiful," Grandmother complimented.

Mother sat at the head of the table and Johnny sat on her right. Grandmother sat across from Johnny, and Grandfather sat next to her. Mother stepped on a little button under the table, which buzzed the kitchen to let Mrs. Jaeger know they were ready to be served.

When Mrs. Jaeger came in with the plate, Johnny asked, "What's that?"

"Artichoke canapés," Mother replied.

"I like artichokes, but this does not look like artichokes."

Johnny stared at two small toasts spread with something pale green in front of him. He leaned forward and smelled his canapés. Grandmother cleared her throat, and Johnny looked up to see eight eyes staring at him. He picked up the toast.

"Where's the can of peas?" He asked.

Mother tried not to laugh. "Canapés is French for small toast."

"I don't like...."

Mother gently tapped his hand. "You love artichoke."

Yes, he liked pulling the leaves off, dipping them in butter and pulling the leaf through his teeth, scraping the 'meaty' part into his mouth. After the leaves were pulled off, he found the artichoke heart underneath. He scraped off the transparent leaves and white hairs then dipped the heart in butter, which dripped off his chin. He might like it.

"I'll try it," he said.

"This is the same, except the hearts are smashed together with other ingredients and spread over the canapés," Mother encouraged.

"Well, I'll have his," Grandfather chimed in.

Johnny took a bite. "Mmm, this is good. It does taste like artichoke."

The next course was served. Mrs. Jaeger ladled chicken soup

with wide noodles and peas into their bowls. Johnny scooted his spoon around the floating peas and hoped no one would notice. The grownups talked, but he was not listening. He thought about the alligator postcard and how much he missed Pop. Roast Lamb with mashed potatoes, more peas, and wheat yeast rolls came to the table next. Johnny took a roll out of the basket and set it on his bread plate next to a butterball. Mrs. Jaeger served a small crystal dish of peaches pickled in vinegar, brown sugar, and cinnamon.

"This is a meal fit for a king!" Grandfather said. "You've outdone yourself, Lizzy! Johnny, pass the mint jelly please."

"Do you need help cutting your meat?" Mother asked.

"No, thank you. I can do it," Johnny picked up the knife in his left hand.

"The other hand," she said.

He corrected himself and cut his meat properly. He lifted his knife to slice the butterball. The knife hit Mother's china plate with a loud *ping* and flipped the butterball across the table. The pale yellow ball of butter landed in Grandmother's peaches. Johnny froze. Grandmother stiffened. Her mouth opened but words did not come out. Mother placed her hand in front of her face and laughed as Grandfather let out a guffaw. Grandmother could be stern at times, especially about table manners and proper etiquette, but even she could not help herself.

"I think this belongs to you." She laughed as she fished the butterball out of her peaches with a spoon.

Mrs. Jaeger ran in, "Is everyone fine?"

"Yes," Mother smiled, "Everything is delicious."

"We rescued a flying butterball," Johnny chimed in.

"Flying butterballs?" Mrs. Jaeger looked confused.

"What's for dessert?" Johnny changed the subject.

"Your favorite--pineapple upside-down cake." Then Mrs. Jaeger looked at Mother. "Shall I serve dessert in the library?"

"My favorite, too," Grandmother added. "Yes, let's go into the library and sit by the fire. My bones are chilled."

Mother poured strong black coffee into demitasse cups. "Johnny, serve the sugar, please."

He picked up sugar cubes with tiny silver tongs.

"One lump or two?" he asked, and dropped them into each cup.

Grandfather stared into his black coffee, stirring with a tiny spoon. He said in a hushed, mysterious voice, "A black river, the Suwannee."

"Suwannee?" Johnny repeated, eager to hear more. "Have you been on the Suwannee River?"

"Yes, in my teen years," said Grandfather. "Plenty of gators in the Suwannee. My father took me on a steamboat through hardwood hammocks and swamps along the wild, winding river. I felt like Dr. David Livingstone exploring the Zambezi River through the jungle of central Africa."

Johnny's eyes got bigger with Grandfather's every word, then asked, "Florida had jungles?"

"You could say that," Grandmother added. "Especially for us, it was like a tropical paradise. My mother had rheumatism and our New England winters were difficult for her. So our physician prescribed a warm climate and the sulphur springs of the Suwannee. The water was so dark you couldn't see down into it, nor imagine, what creatures lay beneath. Then, as if something sacred, the river became clear and pure at the springs." Grandmother waved her hand over the coffee cup, "It was mystical."

"Your mother could've stayed here and bathed in the White River," Grandfather said with sarcasm.

"Stop being a skeptic," she scorned him. "Naaman said the same thing to Elisha's messenger in the Old Testament. Elisha sent word to Naaman to bathe in the Jordan River seven times for healing. Naaman complained about traveling to the Jordan, when he could have bathed in the Damascus River instead. Elisha's command was not about the healing of the Jordan; it was about Naaman's faith and obedience to do it. So Naaman did as Elisha told him, and he was healed. My mother was faithful and obedient, so we all went to the springs. The Indian tribes before us also came to the springs for healing."

Grandfather raised a doubtful eyebrow and questioned. "Well, was she healed?"

Grandmother defended, "My mother definitely felt better afterwards!"

"Did you ever see any Indians?" Johnny asked.

"No, that was before our time. After the Seminole Wars, the Seminole Indians were relocated to the Everglades." Grandmother continued, "But I did see an alligator! There were so many people packed on the steamer, my father took me to the top deck so I could have a better view. I saw people pointing to a log, only it wasn't a log... It was an alligator! Florida was the closest thing to a jungle I'll ever see, but there were no Indians."

"Grandfather, did you fight in the Seminole Wars?" John asked.

"No," Grandfather chuckled. "I was born much later, during the Civil War. The settlers who had moved into Florida were greedy for more land. They pushed the Seminoles into the central area, and that was when trouble really started. The closest I ever came to an Indian was at the Smithsonian. George Catlin painted a portrait of Osceola wearing his white plume. I read Catlin described Osceola as 'a gallant fellow who grieved with a broken spirit' after his capture. It was amazing to me Osceola allowed Catlin to paint his picture."

Grandfather recanted his trips on the railways, which brought many northern tourists to the southern tropics. He had stories of hunting trips abroad the steamers, of hunters who shot white egrets and herons for their plumes, panthers, and occasionally, a pioneer's stray cow, or a Florida alligator just because he was there, sunning himself on a muddy bank. Once upon a time, the Indians canoed the rivers and farmed the land peacefully. Then the settlers came and pushed them into the swamps, where they lived among dangerous reptiles.

Johnny asked, "Is that progress, Grandfather?"

"I guess you could say that," Grandfather answered.

Pop had explained progress to him when he said, "Progress can change the landscape and the ways of the people in it. Once that happens, man cannot turn back; he must act wisely."

"Your Pop is a wise man," Grandfather winked. "That's why I gave him a job when he married your mother."

"Johnny, it's getting late," Mother said. "It's your bed time."

"Please, Mother, one more story," Johnny begged.

"When you think about it, phosphate mining is an example of progress changing the land," Grandfather stated.

"What is phosphate used for?" Jonny asked.

"Fertilizer, for one thing," Grandfather responded. "Most of the world's export came from Florida. Everybody was jumping on the wagon, including me. In 1884, hard rock phosphate was discovered in Marion and Citrus County. I bought my land for a dollar an acre and started my phosphate company. Phosphate companies were springing up all over the state; we had 'white fever'. I guess you could say," he chuckled. "We were like prospectors out west who had gold fever. We mined in open pits with picks and shovels. My pit ran into ground water, and filled up. It wasn't good for mining after that, but I still had the land, so we had somewhere to go in the winter."

Grandfather reached over and grabbed the fire poker. He stoked the flowing embers. "The embers remind me of the eyes of the tawny colored panther," he whispered. "Once I was on an excursion and saw her in my spyglass. For the first time, I felt like an intruder. This was her home, and I was standing in her parlor uninvited."

"A panther?" What other wild animals have…" Johnny started to ask.

Mother interrupted, "Johnny it's late. You need to go to bed. No more stories. Tell your grandparents goodnight."

"Good-night," he hugged the three of them. He left the room and walked up stairs with heavy, slow steps. He sat on the top landing and listened.

Margaret listened, then whispered, "I received a long letter from John. He's trying to convince me to move to Florida and live on the farm with him."

Grandfather said, "Yes, I sold him that piece of property. It has hardwood, scrub pine, palmettos and lakefront. I never thought much about it being a farm."

"Is it near your place?" Mother asked.

"A few miles, not far. I thought it might be a good investment for my daughter and grandson someday."

"He wrote he had finished the house and a barn," Mother sighed. "He wants Johnny to help him plant a citrus grove this summer. Can you imagine?"

"Oh, wouldn't that be wonderful for him?" Grandmother suggested.

"But permanently, Mother?" She swallowed hard.

"But you love our winter home," Grandmother added.

"Mother, I cannot do that--not all year round. This is my home. My studio is here. I want Johnny to attend school here," Margaret insisted.

"An orange grove?" Grandfather asked. "I didn't know he wanted to get into the citrus business. It's true; citrus has picked up some since the freeze of twenty-six, which put a lot of growers out of business. It's risky," he continued. "He'll be at the mercy of Mother Nature. I guess that never stops a man from trying."

"Not to mention hurricanes," Grandmother added. "Remember those big ones? They practically wiped the state off the map!"

Investors can't trust the Florida market right now, that's for sure." Grandfather shook his head.

Grandmother asked, "What did you tell him, dear?"

She already knew the answer. Her daughter was a modern, independent woman of the new century. There were very few women sculptors, and she had found her place among them. She was close enough to the galleries in New York. An ocean liner easily traveled Europe every few years when she studied in Paris or went to an exhibition. She had been a member of the women's suffrage movement. Because of her daughter and hundreds like her, women could vote. Women were slowly making their gifts and talents known to the world. Grandmother was proud of her.

Mother squared her shoulders, straightened her back and said, "We'll keep a long distance relationship. I've agreed to let Johnny spend the summer down there."

"Have you told him yet?" Grandmother asked, concerned.

"No, not yet," Margaret said. "It has been hard on Johnny that his father has been gone so long."

Johnny listened at the top of the stairs, like he always did. When he heard his mother's words, his heart sank and his stomach tightened. He thought, *Another 'Not yet'. 'Not yet' spring, 'not yet' knowing the truth...*

"You need to tell him soon," Grandmother insisted.

A burn rushed to his face. He jumped from the landing, ran to his room, and slammed the door.

The grown-ups looked at each other when they heard him.

"Oh, no!" Margaret's heart ached. "He must have been listening."

Grandfather and Grandmother got up together. "We'll say goodbye. You need to go to him."

"Thank you for a wonderful dinner," Grandmother kissed her. "We'll see ourselves out."

Mother held onto the oak handrail and walked up to Johnny's room with soft, quiet steps. She knocked on the door.

"Go away!" He yelled.

She found him under his blankets fully clothed, his pillow dampened from tears.

"Everyone hates me in this family!" he hit his pillow with a clenched fist.

"Johnny, we need to talk," Mother whispered. "No one hates you. We all love you. I am sorry you overheard our conversation. I was going to talk to you about it."

She wanted to touch him--rub his back, but she kept her hands in her lap. "I'm really sorry."

43

The silence between them seemed to last a long time. "Maybe it's my fault," Mother said. "Pop built a small house and barn. He wants to plant an orange grove... that's not for me."

"Don't you love us?" Johnny whimpered.

"That's not a fair question. Of course I love you, but I'm an artist. My work is here, near the city." She cleared her throat, "Would you like to spend the summer with Pop?"

"Do you mean it?" He asked.

"You can take the train," she smiled.

"By myself?" John asked.

"You're old enough. The porters can watch out for you. You'll be fine," she answered. Her back and shoulders stiffened as she said this. She knew she had to let him go.

"It won't be the same. We won't be together," Johnny complained. "What about you, Mother?"

"I'll be okay. I have my studio and volunteer work. I'll miss you terribly; without question."

"Did Pop lose his job? Johnny asked.

"He didn't lose it as much as he gave it up. I think this is the right time for him. He wants to follow his dream. I understand that more than anyone," Mother said. She pulled him towards her; postcards stuck to his shirt. "You have quite a collection, here."

Several weeks later, another postcard arrived in the mail with a picture of Osceola holding a rabbit and returning to his son. He turned it over and read Pop's graphite words.

Osceola walked on our farm!

Osceola walked on our farm!

Chapter Five

The last day of school finally arrived, and it was time for his long awaited trip. Johnny did not pack much.

"Pop will take you shopping for farm clothes," Mother told him.

He could hardly wait to take off his scratchy wool knickers in Florida.

Mother drove him into New York City. Johnny saw men lined up around buildings and down city blocks waiting for food or jobs. The men gazed into the street, waiting for something good to happen. For the first time, Johnny was glad Pop was not home or he might have been standing in line, too.

"Here's the 'Pennsy'," Mother said.

Johnny looked up at the eagles perched on Pennsylvania Station like sentinels guarding travelers. He, his parents, and grandparents had come here many times to take the night trains south for winter. As they walked through the concourse, sunlight streamed through the skylights above the long waiting room. Rows of arched, steel girders framed the entrance to the station's twenty-one tracks. Mother stopped to read the track indicator, which directed them downstairs to the southbound trains. They held onto the brass banister descending to the tracks below. The light from upstairs trickled into the dim underground illuminating a few dark silhouettes. Not as many people traveled south that time of year or could afford to, but still the trains made their routes with fewer travelers.

A Seaboard Air Line Railway's black locomotive sat outside in the yard, while the dark green, steel cars lined up behind it in the station. Johnny breathed in the metallic, dank smells of the underground. He was happy to know the engineer, the conductor, and the Pullman porter still had their jobs on the train.

A uniformed conductor bellowed in a tenor voice, "Maryland, Wash-ing-ton-Dee-Cee! Vir-gin-ia! Car-o-linas! Georgia! *Flo-ree-da!*"

States were sung in rhythmic blues and heard above the clamor of metal, muffled voices, and concourse echoes. Johnny climbed aboard the sleeper car to ride this night train to Tampa.

Mother spoke to a thin, well dressed Negro man in a navy blue tailored uniform. He was known as a Pullman porter. Johnny saw his reflection six times in the porter's shiny brass buttons.

"My son's traveling alone," she said.

"Yes, ma'am," said the courteous porter. "We'll take good care of him."

She turned toward her son and tucked his ticket into his top pocket, kissing him on the cheek.

"I can handle this, Mother," Johnny said.

"I know you can." She reached into her handbag and handed the porter twenty-five cents.

"Thank you," he said slipping it into his pocket.

Johnny thought Mother might have been his best tipper on the train. She stepped down and stood on the platform to watch. She knew he would be all right, but it was not easy letting him go.

"Right this way young man." The porter took Johnny's small leather suitcase, "You can sit here."

He gestured to the middle of the car where two empty seats faced each other. The inside of the car was the same dark green as the outside; even the curtains were green. Johnny sat down, lowered the window, and waved to his mother. She waved back.

The engine was hooked up to electric lines, which heaved its passenger cars out of the station. The train's wheels scraped and squealed against steel tracks of the railway. Once the train rolled into sunlight, he squinted from the bright light. He no longer could see Mother waving her handkerchief. He swallowed hard to move the lump out of his throat. Then the electrical line released the engine as it puffed black smoke. It was on its own, and so was he.

The engine slowly transported its passengers over a network of tracks until it left the city. He loved the sound when the train picked up speed and declared its rhythmic pattern of clicks and clacks. The scene out his window changed from skyscrapers to factories, row houses to neighborhoods, and small towns to countryside along the eastern coast.

In the evening, the steward came into his sleeping car and called for the dinner hour seating. Johnny was hungry and dined alone during the first seating. He sat across from an empty chair and table setting. He had an extra place at the table for Pop, just like at home. He opened a small black leather coin case Mother gave him and counted out his change. The steward gave him a menu, a checklist, and a pencil to write in what he wanted for his dinner. He ordered a cup of consommé, lamb chop with diced potatoes, carrot sticks, and, for dessert, a scoop of vanilla ice cream. He counted out two quarters, a dime, and one nickel to pay for his meal.

When the steward called the second seating for dinner he moved back to his sleeper car. The porter had already pulled down his berth and made it with sheets, pillow, and blanket then hung two heavy curtains for privacy. Johnny climbed up into the upper berth and took his shoes off, placing them in the corner.

"Call if you need anything," then the porter pulled the curtain closed. "Good night." Johnny lay awake with excitement, tomorrow he would see Pop, but soon the rhythm of the rails rocked him to sleep. The next day, he awoke to daylight peering through a slit between the drawn curtains.

A swift sweep opened the curtain, "Good morning!" the porter said cheerfully. He had been up before dawn ready to serve the passengers in his car. "By the time you eat breakfast I'll make up this berth. Tampa won't be long."

"Thank you," said Johnny as he hopped down.

He washed in the men's bathroom at the end of the car and then passed through several cars, following the smell of strong coffee into the dining car. He sat at the same table and checked off cinnamon toast and a cup of tea on the breakfast menu. He pulled another quarter from his coin case. By the time he returned to his sleeping car, the berth was made up, just as the porter had said, and the seats faced each other once again. It was not long before the train rolled into Tampa Union Station. Johnny saw palm trees and smelled salt water mixed with train smoke.

The conductor walked through the cars announcing, "Tampa. Next stop St. Petersburg, Sarasota!" The brakes screeched the train to a stop. "All passengers for Tampa."

"I'm here!" He exclaimed.

"Bye. Watch your step." The tall porter with six shiny brass buttons handed Johnny his satchel.

"Thank you," Johnny jumped off the train and looked down the platform.

John stood with hands in his pockets looking up and down the train for his son. He wore a Panama straw hat and a cotton short-sleeved shirt, rolled taut around his muscular, tan arms.

"Pop, Pop! I'm over here," he yelled.

"Johnny!" Pop waved.

Johnny's legs could not run fast enough. Pop lifted him in the air and gave him a big bear hug. Johnny was surprised at Pop's strength when he lifted Johnny higher than he had remembered. He hugged Pop back as hard as he could.

"I've missed you, son." Pop said, planting his feet back on the ground.

"Me, too!" Johnny smiled.

"What do you have on?" Pop teased, "Before we leave Tampa, we're going to buy you some farm boy clothes."

Johnny laughed. 'Farm boy'--he liked the sound of that. He knew he wanted to be a farm boy. One thing for sure; he would never be bored.

He looked out the window. "Hey, those buildings are on one of my postcards!" Johnny exclaimed.

"Yes, that's the old Tampa Bay Hotel. Your grandparents used to stay there years ago when it was a winter resort. They've turned it into the new University of Tampa. I'm glad to see the buildings are being preserved."

They shopped at Montgomery Ward and bought some cotton plaid shirts with two pockets, denim shorts, a pair of jeans, and a pair of canvas sneakers.

"Can I change now, Pop?"

Even new clothes would feel less scratchy than what he had on. Pop paid for the clothes.

"He'll wear the new clothes out."

The sales lady smiled. "Here's a bag for his old clothes, and the other outfit is in this bag."

"Thank you, ma'am."

When Johnny walked out of the changing room, Pop said, "Much better!"

He did feel much better in his farm boy clothes. "I'm hungry," Johnny complained. "I only ate cinnamon toast on the train."

"Sure, I know just the place."

They headed over to Morrison Cafeteria for supper. Johnny had never seen so much food laid out at once.

"Eat well. When we get home, we've got chores to do." Pop told him.

Johnny could not resist the desserts so he took two--sweet potato, and pecan pie. They both ate until they were filled up and could not eat another bite. Then they headed northwest for home.

Pop made the ride back to the farm suspenseful when he said, "I've got a surprise for you."

Johnny tried to guess what the surprise might be, but he never did get it right. The windows were rolled down so the sound of the wind and road made talking difficult to hear.

"It sure is hot," Johnny yelled. His legs were stuck to the bench seat of the truck.

"I heard this might be the hottest June on record so far," Pop yelled back.

Johnny stuck his arm out the window to see if the breeze felt cooler, it was not. "Is that a swamp?"

"It's the Withlacoochee, your first clue!" Pop smiled.

"What did you say?" Johnny asked.

"I said, 'We'll be home soon; it'll be a few degrees cooler in the shade."

Chapter Six

Pop turned left off the main road. They headed south, crossing railroad tracks on to a dirt road named Moccasin Slough. They drove through woods of wild pine and Blackjack, with a few scrub palmettos and scattered live oaks.

"Our place starts right about here," Pop pointed out the window. Soon he turned down a narrow lane lined with newly planted water oaks. "I planted these this winter. They look like twigs now, but they'll get big."

"Do we have any neighbors?" Johnny asked. He did not see another house or farm along the way.

"Sure we do. There're folks further down the slough," Pop assured him.

Oscee greeted them wagging his tail when the truck pulled in front of the pole barn with a tin roof.

"Hi, boy. Good dog. Pop, what's his name? You didn't tell me we had a dog," Johnny said with great excitement.

"This is Oscee. Oscee, this is Johnny," Pop introduced.

"Is he the surprise?" Johnny asked. "Where did you get him from?"

"Oh, I guess I have quite a few surprises. He found me, and

we've been friends ever since. He's good company."

Pop whistled for Oscee to follow. "Come on, boy. Let's show Johnny around."

"Where did his name come from?" Johnny asked. "Oscee?"

Oscee panted. His tongue stretched toward the ground to keep cool.

"He's named after Osceola, the Seminole chief."

"Is that what you meant on the postcard, 'Osceola walked on our farm'?"

"No, I meant the real Osceola," Pop laughed. "But that's funny, I never thought of that."

"How do you know he did?" Johnny asked.

"Ol' timers have been telling me stories about the Second Seminole War and the battle which took place around here. I've been doing a little reading on my own, too," Pop said. "I'll show you later, but right now we have work to do."

They walked into the barn, but it was not much cooler inside. Johnny had to adjust his eyes after being in the bright sunshine. There was room for a truck, a John Deere tractor, and a workbench. There was a small room for supplies, a cooler, storage for hay, and two stalls. Pop went out to the paddock to call his Jerseys in.

"I milk twice a day and keep my evening milk in a cooler. Then I milk again in the morning, early. Tomorrow you can help me with my route before the milk spoils. I sell it for twelve cents a quart. They get fourteen at the grocer." Pop pulled up his three-legged milking stool and pail as if he had always done it.

The red-brown Jersey with dark brown circles around her eyes mooed gently and swayed her tail to rid herself of flies.

"This is Magnolia. Magnolia, this is Johnny," Pop introduced.

Johnny watched Pop squirt milk from Magnolia's teat into a metal pail. Several Jersey cows waited in the small paddock for their turn in the stalls.

"Jerseys can handle the Florida heat better than other breeds," Pop added. "A fellow in the next county needed to sell, so I offered to buy his cows and a few heifers."

Pop knew about Jerseys. He had spent his childhood on his grandparents' dairy farm. It was the Citrus business he had to learn.

"Over there," he nodded, "I've got another surprise for you."

Johnny saw a Jersey calf, the color of cinnamon, curled up asleep in the hay. He asked, "Is it a boy or a girl?"

"It's a bull calf."

"Hi, little fella." Johnny leaned down to him and gently rubbed the curly bangs on his forehead. The calf woke up, sleepy-eyed and wobbly-legged, to greet the stranger. He nudged Johnny with his wet pink nose and sucked his fingers.

"Oh slimy!" He wiped his hand on his shirt.

"He's hungry, son. You can feed him."

Pop had made a nipple from a piece of hose pushed through a hole in a metal pail. He poured in Magnolia's warm milk while the calf forcefully nudged the pail.

"Whoa, fella," Johnny laughed. "You're going to pull this right out of my hands."

Oscee licked up the spilled milk.

"Thanks, Os!"

The calf sucked and butted the pail for more.

"There's more, here you go."

There was a lot of excitement his first day. It was hard for him to believe he woke up on a train that morning and then there he was, in Pop's barn feeding a calf. Bats flew out of the barn and mosquitoes buzzed around Johnny's ear.

The sun had gone down by the time they finished their chores, but it did not feel any cooler at dusk. The air was still and sultry in the lamp-lit kitchen.

"Wash up in the basin, son. I'll put supper out."

Johnny splashed water on his arms, neck and face. He felt refreshed when salted perspiration rolled off him. Then Pop served cold biscuits, sausage and a tall glass of Magnolia's fresh milk.

"Let's get you settled," Pop said and took Johnny's bags into his new room. He fell asleep to the croaks of bullfrogs, *Jug-o-rum, jug-o-rum.*

It was still dark in Johnny's room when he awoke the next morning. The lake looked like a mirror reflecting the first faint light of dawn. He hung his bare feet over the edge of the bed and slid his toes on the smooth wood floor. He wiggled them, happy; he would not need shoes or socks for the whole summer. He put on the new pair of shorts and a cotton, plaid, short-sleeved shirt with two pockets.

Pop was already in the kitchen making breakfast.

"Good morning, son. You're up early. It's going to be a hot one today. We better get our chores done." Pop put out a bowl of cold melon from the icebox and hard-boiled eggs. "Here, have some orange juice. I squeezed it myself. It's a late orange, called a Valencia."

"It's delicious." Johnny had never seen Pop so handy in the kitchen, nor doing chores, or milking. He loved Pop, but he had to get used to this new father before him.

When they stepped outside. Pop reached in his pocket and took out a handkerchief to wipe the sweat dripping from his brow. "Yes sir, it's going to be a hot one." Johnny had never seen Pop sweat before either, especially standing still.

Oscee was still asleep. His four legs hung over the porch edge like a melted dog.

"Come Os," Pop whistled. "To the barn."

Oscee stood up slowly and gave a long stretch before he stepped off the porch. The morning air was wet and heavy. Johnny heard moisture dripping on palmettos fronds beneath the trees.

"Is it raining?" he asked holding up his hand.

"No, just heavy dew," Pop replied.

The dampness on Johnny's skin made him feel cool and sticky at the same time. He followed the shadowy figures of Pop and Oscee barefoot.

"Ouch!" He picked up his foot and felt …"Ow, this is prickly!"

Then pulled it out of his skin.

"Sand spurs. You're going to have to toughen up those tender feet of yours," Pop laughed. "Have you thought of a name for your calf yet?"

"No, sir," Johnny said as he took the pail off its hook.

After they finished milking, Pop showed Johnny how to reach under the warm bellies of the red hens to collect eggs. "We sell these, too, on our morning route. This'll be a good way for you to meet folks around here," Pop said.

The morning heated up even more by the time they had finished their route and returned to the farm. He did not want to admit it, but he was ready for a nap.

"I'm thirsty," Johnny said.

Pop poured water for them to drink. They sat in the shade on the front porch.

"Whew! What's that smell?" Johnny said, alarmed, when Pop handed him the glass. "Smells like rotten eggs!"

"You'll get used to it. Sulphur in the water. Taste better colder. It took me awhile to get used to it but now I love the taste of it. You can't get this up the country."

Johnny held his nose as he drank. He was not sure he would get used to it, but he did not say that. He spent the next few days exploring their farm covered with areas of scrub palmettos, wild magnolia, pine trees, and oaks.

When Pop showed him the land he had cleared he said, "This clearing is where we're going to plant our grove. I like the sound of that, 'The Clearing'. I think that's what we'll name our farm. I've ordered grafted seedlings of Hamlin--an early fruit, Valencia; a late orange, Navels; and some Marsh grapefruit, which are ready to be picked up. I can't wait to smell their first blossoms. You should've smelled them this spring from the groves across the lake."

The next week, they drove to a citrus nursery in Manatee County to pick up their seedlings. Pop borrowed a stack truck, which had a bigger bed than his pickup. On the way to the nursery, Johnny saw truck farms, which harvested lettuce and tomatoes during the winter months. He saw orange groves, which stretched for miles in all directions--rows and rows of lush, dark green trees. Some of them still had oranges hanging from their branches. He noticed one grove had trucks, with ladders and pickers harvesting the last of late-season fruit. When they pulled into the nursery a man led them to their order.

Johnny took one look and said, "These are trees, Pop? They look like sticks to me."

"I know they don't look like much now," Pop replied. "But they're healthy fruit trees grafted on a sour orange root stock. They'll grow into beautiful, lush trees bearing white-gold grapefruit and yellow-gold oranges about five years from now."

"Five years?" Johnny asked with disappointment.

Five years was a long time. The seedlings' roots were wrapped with burlap to keep them moist until they could be planted. Men loaded them into the truck, then they headed home, to 'The Clearing'.

"Son, we are officially in the citrus business," Pop smiled. "Partner?"

"Partner." Johnny shook his hand. "It's a deal."

The next morning, Pop said, "We're going to start planting our grove. Mr. Emil is coming, and he'll bring some help with him."

Johnny watched from his perch in the old, twisted oak. A cloud of dust billowed like a giant dust ball rolling down Moccasin Slough. The cloud disappeared when the black Model A pickup stopped. Mr. Emil stepped out of his truck, chewing on a short stogie and wearing denim overalls and a white T-shirt stained with sweat.

"Well, look who's here," Pop waved. "Perfect timing!"

"Mornin' boys," he said in a cheerful, robust, southern drawl and shook their hands with a firm grip.

"It's good to meet you, Johnny. Miss Sadie told me she met you when you helped yo' Daddy with his deliverin'."

"Mr. Emil and I have known each other a long time. He worked for your grandfather's phosphate company," Pop explained.

"'Do some truck farming now. I help Doc with his new grove in Floral City. Yes, I see I'm just in time," Mr. Emil said.

His rough, sun leathered hand tousled the boy's blond hair. Johnny realized at that moment he had not combed it since the summer started, and no one really cared if he did or not.

"Yer, lookin' a little pale," Mr. Emil laughed heartily. "It won't be long 'fore you'll get some color in yer cheeks, and then you'll start lookin' like a Florida Cracker!"

"A Cracker?" Johnny asked. "What's a Cracker?"

"I meant you'd look like me, I'm a Cracker. My kin go back to the first colonists who came down from Georgia. They were pioneers in these back woods. Just like pioneers out west, white settlers had trouble with the Indians. Same thing here; settlers wanted to get Indians off the land. After the Second Seminole War, my kinfolk settled in this county. They had scrub cows--not like the pretty things your daddy has," he winked. "They were scrawny boned and had horns. Why, when I was a young'un, they roamed free in the hammock. They always had moss hangin' from their horns. Once, my Granddaddy was madder than a hornet when he found one of his cattle shot down by the river. Probably a huntin' party the steamers brought down on the Withlacoochee."

"Speaking of the Withlacoochee--after we finish our planting, I plan to take Johnny on a canoe trip on the river. Do you think you can run a shuttle for us?" Pop asked.

"Glad to," Mr. Emil responded.

Another truck pulled into the clearing with men Mr. Emil hired from town. From that day on, they worked harder than Johnny thought possible. They dug small holes in the sandy soil and filled them with water before setting in the seedlings. Johnny's favorite job was filling the holes with water. In the heat of the day, he poured water on himself to cool off. Rows of saplings were set into their own little pool of water and covered with sand. While the men went onto the next seedling, Johnny built a little dike around each one to hold the water in. For several days, they planted seedlings after the morning milking, worked until the bats flew at dusk, and then milked again. Tired and weary, they ate light suppers and fell into bed exhausted.

What would Mother think if she knew he fell into bed with his clothes on and dirty feet? He was so exhausted, even the sunburn on his neck and arms could not keep him awake. He fell asleep listening to bull frogs and deep bellows of alligators in the distance. One day, the last tree was planted, the last dike was made, and the last pool of water was poured. The cleared field had been planted with rows of little sticks.

Pop kept his promise--a river journey on the Withlacoochee. Johnny's eyelids were pried open by a bright orange light. The sun had risen above the lake and peeked through the lacy branches outside his window. He took his finger and placed it over the orange disc. In a few minutes the sun rose above his finger. His eyes popped as the sun cast orange flames across the water. He yelled and leaped out of the bed.

"Pop let me sleep in!"

He ran to the barn, where Pop had already loaded the milk on the truck.

"Mornin' sleepy head! Just in time for the route."

"You didn't wake me!"

"You need your rest if you're going to help me canoe the Withlacoochee."

The two of them drove their route, and Johnny sprinted at each stop of the delivery; there was no time to visit.

Once they returned to the farm, Pop walked to the lake front, where his red wooden canoe leaned against a Live Oak. He hoisted it over his head, and flipped it on his Ford Model A truck bed.

"Here, Son, catch," he tossed the rope over to Johnny. "Tie it on the other side."

Pop checked the ropes. "Nice and tight, we don't want to lose her on the road."

They packed a picnic of peaches, cold beef on biscuits, and a container of lemonade.

"Before we leave, I've something to show you," Pop said. "Come over here."

Next to a small brick fireplace, there was a narrow bookshelf Pop called his "Florida Library." He had issues of the historical periodical, "Florida Historical Quarterly," and a few history books he had collected over the years.

"Look at this," he said as he flipped through the pages of a 1925 volume of the Quarterly. "This is a copy of an 1840 map of Florida at the end of the Second Seminole War."

He held a magnifying glass for Johnny over the Withlacoochee River. Pop put his finger at the river's beginnings in the south, following it north and then west to the Gulf of Mexico.

"This is Fort Brooke," he pointed on the map. "What town is that now?"

Johnny read the words "Tampa Bay" through the magnifier. "It must be Tampa?"

"Yes. If we follow this wagon road north, cross the river, and head northeast, we come to Fort King, which is now Ocala. A wagon road also goes north to Fort Drane. This area is the cove of the Withlacoochee, where the Seminoles settled. The Indians felt the white man had broken their promise and thought the White Father had no right to sell land that didn't belong to them."

Johnny read the forts listed on the map aloud. "Fort Drane, Fort King, Fort Cooper, Fort McClure, Fort Dade, Fort Cross, and Fort Brooke." Then he noticed X's and asked, "What are the X's for?"

"Battles," Pop read, "Dade's Battle', December twenty-eighth, 1835. That's what really started the war. Clinch's battle, December thirty-first, 1835, and Gaines's Battle, February twenty-seventh, 1836."

"This looks like a treasure map!" Johnny exclaimed.

"In a way, you're right," Pop said and pointed at the map. "Even though this map denotes these main battles along the river, there were other battles also fought nearby or in the same locations. The only road was this wagon road which went through dense hammock and palmettos."

"You mean like the swamp and palmettos behind our paddock?" Johnny asked.

"Pretty close. I've read letters, which described the Florida territory like a 'jungle', to most northern soldiers, it must've been. Here's another map you might find interesting." Pop unfolded a larger Florida map dated 1921. "What do you notice about this map?"

Johnny looked at it carefully. "Here's the Withlacoochee, Tampa, Ocala, and names of towns… The lakes are in different places."

"What else?" Pop asked.

"The X's are gone--no battles and forts." Johnny asked, "What happened to them?"

"Good observation, son. It's like they've disappeared, but they can't be erased from history. In fact, the year this map was made, the state set aside funds to protect the site of the Dade Battlefield as a memorial, but it's not marked on here. We're going to drive south and put our canoe in here," he pointed. "Near Croom. Hopefully, someday the maps will have X's again to mark these places; so generations will know what happened here."

"What did happen?" Johnny wondered.

He imagined himself a young Jim Hawkins in search of a pirate's buried treasure. Instead of setting sail in a ship on the high seas, they were taking their voyage on a river in a red wooden canoe.

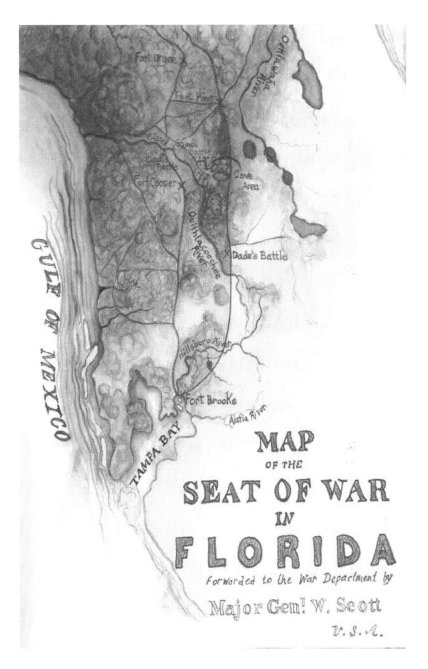

Copy of map of Florida at the end of the Second Seminole War

MURIEL TUTTLE EDEN-PAUL

Chapter Seven

Johnny sat in the bow as Pop pushed off from the grassy bank and rocked the canoe. Oscee sat in the middle, and Pop sat in the stern. At first, the canoe floated with the current of the river. Pop began to paddle, stroking the water on one side and then the other. He lifted the paddle horizontally; then sliced the river again. He taught Johnny to paddle the opposite side of him until they were in sync with one another.

The red wooden canoe traveled the river framed by lush cypress trees. Their roots grew up and looked like knobby knees poking through the water. From a distance, the trees overhead looked like they reached across the river and touched one another. When they moved closer, Johnny looked up into blue sky as the river separated gum trees, hickory, and oaks draped with Spanish moss and vines. The sky reflected in the dark water, except areas with thick blankets of floating water hyacinths.

The canoe parted the plants, leaving a dark trail behind them. Johnny looked behind at the path they had just made. He reached into the water and pulled up a plant. The leaves were oval with a mass of black hairy roots, which dripped river water on his knees. He squeezed the bulb shaped stalk. It felt spongy and popped between his fingers.

"What's this? They're everywhere," he said.

"Those are water hyacinth," Pop answered. "They're more like a water weed. I heard a story once; a lady brought them here in the 1880s from her travels to South America. She thought they had pretty flowers. They've grown like wildfire ever since and are a big problem."

Just then, they noticed some men in a boat breaking up a hyacinth jam.

"Hey, there!" They waved, "Makin' it through okay?"

"Yes, thank you," Pop said. "See, they hired boatmen to clear the river because the drifts are so thick, boats can't get through. It's hard to imagine a time when they were not clogging the river," Pop said thoughtfully. "When the Seminoles and U.S. Army battled here, they had enough troubles with war but they didn't have water hyacinth."

Johnny squinted to look down the river along the banks. Hyacinths were packed so tightly together, it looked as though a person could walk across them. "What would the river look like without them?"

"Look over to your right. Do you see that 'gator? He's a big one, maybe twelve feet," Pop said.

Oscee barked and barked.

"Quiet Os," Pop scolded, "or you'll be his lunch."

"Pop, don't say that," Johnny whispered.

"It's true; gators like nothing better than 'dog' picnic."

Oscee looked at Pop and John, tilting his ears from one side to the other. He quietly laid his head down on his paws on the bottom of the canoe.

"I think he understood you," Johnny whispered. "Grandfather told me people used to shoot the gators from the steamboats on their hunting trips. It's just sitting there minding its own business."

As the canoe floated by, the alligator pushed its heavy body off the bank into the water. It did not make a splash, but the hyacinth bobbed up and down in its wake. It could have been anywhere beneath the dark water. Johnny sat still. Goosebumps formed on his arms when he heard something scrape under the canoe. Maybe it was an old dead branch, or it could have been the gator.

"Once there was a Seminole chief named Alligator," Pop said. "It was a fitting name because he was as tough and protective of his Florida as a mother gator is of her babies. His other name was 'Haplatter Tushenuggee'."

"Chief Alligator is easier to say," Johnny said. "I'd rather be called Alligator. Where did that gator go?"

"I'm not sure," Pop said. "Maybe we should pull over beneath this bald cypress to eat."

"Good idea. I'm hungry," Johnny agreed.

"Canoeing sure builds up an appetite," Pop handed him his beef and biscuits.

"Mmm, It taste good!" Johnny noticed tracks in the mud around the base of the cypress knees. "What made these? They look like little hands."

"Raccoon," Pop answered. "He probably hunted frogs for his supper last night."

Johnny reached down and scooped up river water to give Oscee a drink. The dark river became clear when cupped in his hands.

"Grandfather described the Suwannee River like the color of black coffee. This river is, too. Why does it look so dark when it's really clear?"

"Rotting plants, river grass, and tannic acid from the cypress. I've read Indians described this river like dusk even during the day. Darker the water, the better, don't you think?"

"Not really," Johnny answered.

"I bet gators and water moccasins think so," Pop teased. "Dark water makes a good hiding place for alligators and water moccasins, just like the swamp was a dark hiding place for Seminoles. The darker--the swampier--the better," Pop chuckled. "You be careful sticking your hands in the water next time. You never know what's hiding under there."

"What do you mean?" Johnny quickly pulled his hands back into the canoe.

"Cottonmouth," Pop pointed to a snake in the water. "Water moccasin. They're poisonous. Do you see it?"

"Yes, sir."

He watched the snake hold its head out of the water. It wove in and around hyacinth as he followed its "Z" trail in open water.

"Weren't Seminoles afraid of alligators and snakes?"

"No, they respected them. They learned to smell poisonous snakes and avoid their territory. Once, Seminoles were farmers in Georgia and North Florida until settlers moved them off their land. They sought refuge in the swamp and the cove of the Withlacoochee and learned to live among its creatures. Runaway slaves joined the Indians, and the cove became a safe haven for them as well."

"What were they hiding from?"

"They didn't want to move to the reservations."

"You mean, like the government moved the Plains Indians to reservations?" Johnny asked.

"Yes," Pop replied. "'President Jackson told his red children that white people are settling around them. Their game would disappear, and they would be poor and hungry. He referred to himself as their father and said he would take care of them, giving them a new home west of the Mississippi, with their brothers in the Creek nation. A few Seminole Chiefs agreed to take a look, but they felt the people were bad there even though the land was good. The journey also would've been too difficult for them. Some chiefs wanted to honor the treaties, but other Seminoles considered them weak, like Osceola, Micanopy, Alligator, and Jumper. They were angry when white men attacked the Seminoles in their encampments. They refused to leave Florida and began to strike back, attacking plantations and settlements. They began to take refuge and hide out in the cove of the Withlacoochee. No one trusted anyone, and each side had their own cause. Osceola hid behind cypress trees watching for his enemy. He could be watching right now."

"Osceola? You sent me a postcard." Johnny's thoughts trailed off with the river current. The picture on the postcard showed Osceola with his son, a Seminole boy about his age.

Johnny said, "I bet Osceola and his son canoed this river together."

"Maybe they did," Pop agreed. "There're probably other things you and the chief's son have in common."

"Like what? I know he didn't eat artichoke canapés."

Pop chuckled. "No, but maybe fishing or catching frogs or swimming."

Johnny thought of another thing they had in common, only he did not say it out loud. Both boys knew what it was like to wait for their fathers to come home.

The canoe drifted as they watched a Great Blue Heron on the shore. It stared in the shallow for its supper and made a low, hoarse sound when their canoe came too close. The heron flew off, its dark branch-like legs hanging heavy beneath it, and dropped a small snake out of its long beak.

"That's what you get. Don't talk with your mouth full," Johnny yelled to the heron and laughed.

"We are very near the 'X' on the map where Dade's battle took place. It wasn't on the river but close by," Pop said, and they continued to drift in the current. "Northeast of here, Major Dade and his men fought the Seminoles December twenty-eighth, 1835. There was a blood bath that day."

Johnny felt a chill down his spine. He looked up and down the bank for anything that would show him where the battle was. "I don't see anything different."

"Maybe it's not what you see but what you hear, son. For some people, what was lost is soon forgotten, but for others knowing the truth is kept right here." Pop pointed toward his son's chest. "The truth about history changes people. It changes the way we think; it should, anyway. We should learn from it--what worked and what didn't."

Johnny heard some birds overhead, an occasional fish jump, and leaves rustled in a gentle breeze, but no sounds of gunfire.

"Fort King and Fort Brooke," Pop continued, "had a handful of soldiers to watch over this region. General Clinch recommended an increase of military force, but President Jackson didn't see a need for it. A couple years before, an Indian Agent, Wiley Thompson was assigned to Fort King to oversee the Seminoles. He began to enforce rules upon them. For example, he refused to sell them alcohol or gunpowder. Unfortunately, when he took away these items and other small gifts to the Indians, it resulted in their hatred of him. Osceola had a plan for him to suffer, and it was coming soon."

"What was Osceola going to do? I feel sorry for them. It was their home first," Johnny said softly.

"Yes, it was, but times had changed, and the food sources for the Seminoles were being used up. Agent Thompson didn't provide the food he promised, so they had to steal food to survive. Even when the government did provide corn, it was too late for the Seminoles. They knew what they had to do," Pop continued. "The meetings between the Seminoles and the government got them nowhere. Neither side listened to the other. One chief by the name of Charley Amathla decided he would rather take his chances out west and wanted to take his people with him. He would either keep his word or die to remain a noble man. Osceola broke off from his group and shot Amathla. The death of Amathla marked a turning point for the Seminoles. They fled their towns and moved their families into the swamp. Their trails were hidden as they took refuge in the cove area of the Withlacoochee River and the chain of lakes known as Tsala Apopka. Thus the outbreak of battles in this area began."

The June sun heated up the cove, and heat waves rippled above the surface of the river. The canoe floated lazily until it bumped into a fallen log. Pop paddled them back into the current. Johnny sat on the floor of the canoe and laid his head in his seat. Water lapped gently around the bow, and a hot breeze lulled him to sleep. The current carried them back in time when the river was a stage for war. The red canoe floated near a battle fought almost one hundred winters ago.

Johnny sat in the bow as Pop pushed off from the grassy bank and rocked the canoe. Oscee sat in the middle, and Pop sat in the stern.

Chapter Eight

Once the news of Chief Charley Amathla reached General Clinch, he knew that he needed more military forces. He ordered a detachment under the command of Major Dade to march from Fort Brooke to Fort King on the twenty-third of December in 1836. They started out slowly four miles from Fort Brooke when the canon being pulled by the oxen broke down. By the time they reached the bridge on the Hillsborough River two days later, it had been burned.

Major Dade commanded, "I need some runners to scout out another crossing. We'll camp here until I get their report."

On the twenty-seventh, they made it about six more miles and crossed the Withlacoochee River. Major Dade ordered Captain Gardiner, "Captain, I'm quite sure our enemies are watching our every move. We must take all necessary precautions against a surprise attack."

The Captain went down his line in command. "We're bedding down here tonight men. No fires!"

Major Dade was right about one thing: the Seminole scouts had followed the soldiers, reporting the military's every move to their leaders. Ironically, the troops had no idea how close they were to the Seminole's hideout in the swamp where plans were being made.

"Our scouts have been out and reported the soldiers' encampment," Alligator said, as Seminole leaders made plans for their attack.

"We need to attack now. They've been on the move for three days and getting closer to our hideout." Jumper said, "We can no longer wait for Osceola to join us."

"I think we should wait for Osceola as planned," a timid Micanopy urged. "Osceola said we were to wait until he returned, and then attack the troops,"

"Old Chief, this is our land, not theirs. We must fight for it. If we don't attack now, it may be too late," Jumper persisted.

"If we meet with defeat," Alligator said, "we can retreat into the swamp. They can't find us there. We'll not leave our home."

"For the rest of you," shouted Jumper, "those who are faint of heart should stay behind. We'll attack in the morning."

The next day, the soldiers woke up to a chilly morning. The men buttoned their overcoats over their ammunition boxes.

"Captain get the men in line to move out. I have already sent my advanced guard ahead of us. However, I've no concern about a daylight attack and surely not in the open," Major Dade said confidently.

As he led the column of 107 men on horseback, he encouraged the soldiers. "Have a good heart; our difficulties and dangers are over now, and as soon as we arrive at Fort King you'll have three days to rest and Christmas gaily."

The commanding officers words did indeed raise the morale of his men. Thoughts of glowing fires and a wild turkey dinner awaiting them warmed the shivering troops from the frosty, damp air.

Meanwhile, the Seminoles draped wool blankets over one shoulder as they prepared to meet Dade and his men. Alligator said, "It's time for us to move out of the swamp and into the pine barren."

Jumper asked Alligator, "How many are there of them?"

Alligator answered, "I counted one hundred and eight."

Then Jumper asked, "How many of us?"

Alligator counted, "One hundred and eighty warriors."

As the warriors approached the road, they could hear the soldiers coming. The approaching troops moved through the palmettos, and Jumper and Alligator signaled to their brothers to hide themselves. The Seminoles did not utter a sound. They were still, hidden behind every tree or tall palmetto. The column was divided into three sections, with gaps between the advance party, main troops, and the rear guard. The Seminoles flanked the road on the west side, and on the east side was a pond.

"How about you, Micanopy? Are you with us?" Jumper challenged the older chief.

"I'll show you." Micanopy took his position behind a pine tree and aimed his gun. "We'll surprise them."

By nine o'clock the command was in the pine barren. Jumper sounded his cry of war.

"Whaaaaoooooop!"

Micanopy fired his gun, and the other warriors shot from behind trees or where they were hidden in the tall grass in rapid fire. A bullet hit Major Dade in the chest and he fell from his horse. Then Captain Fraser fell from his. The Seminoles' strategy was to kill the officers first. After the first firing from the concealed warriors, half the soldiers were dead, their bodies left in the sun.

Captain Gardiner, who headed up another column of troops, knew a disaster had happened when he saw Major Dade's horse return without his rider. He hardly had time to process the event when shots fired from the enemy. After about an hour of fighting, the Indians began gathering together as if retreating. Alligator said, "We'll go back to the swamp. I think they're dead."

"Build a breastwork! Now!" the Captain shouted. His men rushed to throw together a triangle of pine about two and half feet high.

A warrior ran towards Alligator and Jumper as they headed back to the swamp, shouting, "There's more! They're building a pen of logs."

Alligator and Jumper returned with about ten warriors firing a second volley from the trees and palmettos, but this time they were advancing. Five hours into the fighting, Captain Gardiner was severely wounded cried out to his men.

"I can give you no more orders lads, do your best!"

When Lieutenant Basinger saw Captain Gardiner fall after a shot to his chest, he said, "I am the only one left boys. We must do the best we can."

The last surviving officer had to assume responsibility and take charge of whoever was left.

"Load the cannon," Lieutenant Basinger yelled. "Fire!"

The six-pounder fired about five or six rounds. The Seminoles dodged the balls behind trees and kept firing.

Alligator shouted, "The smoke has cleared. There are more of them dead. I think we killed them all."

Jumper and Alligator and the others approached the pine logs. Lieutenant Basinger, severely wounded saw the men approaching. "They're coming this way, Private Clark, lie down and pretend yourself to be dead."

Alligator and Jumper looked into the boxes.

"They have no powder!" Alligator said. "Step inside the pen, see if anyone still lives."

As soon as they did, Lieutenant Basinger found enough strength to grab an Indian. He was a brave man; even the Seminoles respected that. Jumper's cousin grabbed the lieutenant's gun and hit him in the head, killing him. Alligator and Jumper quietly stepped around the dead bodies, gathering the weapons.

Jumper said, "Let's go back to the swamp and wait for Osceola. We'll report to him about our day. We killed them all, but we only lost three warriors."

They returned to their home in the swamp with five wounded men.

In the afternoon of the same day, Osceola and the other warriors knew that Fort King had been left with only a few soldiers. Two other companies, which were posted there, had marched to Fort Drane. Agent Wiley Thompson and Lieutenant Constantine Smith walked in the pinewoods after their meal, near the sutler's house. The sound of war whoops bounced off the trees and vibrated the still afternoon, followed by gunfire. Fourteen bullets fatally hit Agent Thompson and two bullets killed Lieutenant Smith. Osceola ran out of the woods and plunged a knife into his enemy, whom he had vowed to kill. Then he ran into the sutler's house outside the picket, throwing furniture and looking for supplies. His shrill yells sent chills down Mr. Roger's cook, who was hidden behind some barrels.

Then the warriors retreated. When the cook came out of hiding she found the sutler, Mr. Rogers, and his clerks dead from gunshots. The few soldiers left to guard the Fort were surprised by the sounds of yells, whoops, gunfire, and the screams of Mr. Roger's cook.

Captain Lendrum exclaimed, "We're being attacked from the woods. I didn't see them get so close. Men, go check the agent's office and the sutler's store house."

The soldiers were too late. The Seminoles had vanished into the woods. Captain Lendrum and his men brought the broken and battered bodies they found back inside the fort.

Later in the night, Osceola joined the rest of the warriors in the Wahoo swamp. Before Alligator or Jumper could report their victory of the morning, they saw their leader's victory strapped around his middle. Scalps were suspended from the waist of their comrades, the victims' blood still dripping from them. The Seminoles danced around their campfire all night, rejoicing in their victory of the day. Their laughter echoed through the swamp as they made fun and mimicked Agent Thompson. Their medicine chief, Illis-Higher-Hadjo, set the scalps on a ten-foot pole while they danced until dawn. While the Seminoles rejoiced and reveled in their victory, one lone private was still alive--barely. Private Clark writhed out from under his dead comrades and crawled through the woods. He was injured and in severe pain, but he managed to get back to Fort Brooke and report the massacre he had witnessed.

Chapter Nine

An officer in the United States Army, General Clinch had served many years of duty in the territory of Florida. He was a gallant and responsible leader of his men as well as his family. Besides his military life, he also owned two plantations--a rice plantation on the coast of Georgia and a sugar cane plantation secluded in the Florida wilderness. The incomes from rice and sugar cane supplemented his army pay to support his wife, Eliz, and their eight children. When he stayed at his Florida sugar plantation, he was a long way from the comforts of his Georgia plantation.

As a plantation owner and general, his two worlds collided at Lang Syne. During the Second Seminole War, he turned his rice plantation into military headquarters to help with the campaign. The living conditions and accommodations supplied by Lang Syne were barely habitable. However, it offered a suitable location for supplies and management of the territory.

General Clinch ordered, "Captain Drane, I want you to build a picket twelve feet high to fortify my buildings."

"Yes, sir." Captain Drane did not lose any time. His men worked, and the sound of their picks, shovels, and axes echoed through the piney-wood. The new fort was completed more quickly than General

Clinch expected, as well as a blockhouse for the combat cannon.

After he inspected the job, he said, "Captain, I'm going to name this fort after you."

Captain Drane saluted, "Yes, sir. Thank you sir."

And so it was that Lang Syne plantation became Fort Drane and another X on the map.

General Clinch predicted the Seminoles would not leave Florida peacefully. It had been a year since he had conferred and negotiated with them. Requests had been sent to Washington for action, more men, and supplies. President Jackson accused Clinch of not doing much to stop the Seminoles from attacking settlements and farms. Clinch felt the government did not understand the problems of the terrain or the Seminoles' love of their homeland. He needed reinforcement.

Brigadier General of the militia, Richard Keith Call, was an answer to his needs. Call left Tallahassee and marched to the Suwannee River, where East Florida volunteers joined him. General Clinch and his small army anxiously awaited the Florida militia, which arrived December twenty-fourth, 1835, at Fort Drane.

General Call commanded a forceful presence when he entered the picket walls. He dismounted his horse and said, "I was riding earlier this month, when a messenger found me and dispatched the news the Indians were uprising. Rest easy, General; the Florida Militia is here!"

"General Call, I appreciate you coming," General Clinch greeted the commander of the volunteers. " I welcome you humbly into the squalid conditions of Fort Drane." He spoke in a soft, hoarse voice. "I've the utmost confidence in your leadership and experience. Washington tells me my inadequate supply of men will be sufficient. They also believe we can negotiate with the Seminoles, so they will move out west. I can tell you, sir, after conferring with them, I predicted our efforts would come to this. I'm grateful the request for more men has finally been recognized by the War Department."

"I arranged several meetings in Tallahassee and two hundred

fifty men volunteered for the campaign. We've got friendly Indians up our way, and Tiger Tail was at the meeting," said General Call.

"Really? Be cautious, sir, sometimes it's difficult to discern the friendly Indians from the rebels." General Clinch warned, "They'll turn against one another, so they'll easily turn against us. I question the loyalty of Tiger Tail at your meeting."

"He seemed friendly," General Call defended. "We haven't had any trouble with him."

"We'll see." General Clinch cleared his throat, pulled out his map, and said, "I organized a plan to concentrate all our forces here."

Boastful, in a loud, powerful voice, General Call added, "We saw Indian activity on our way here. The volunteers are quite confident."

"I've also ordered Major Dade to march two companies to join us from Fort Brooke," Clinch continued.

"Sir, are you not concerned by the severity of this situation?" Call scoffed.

"Of course I am. No one knows the Indians better than I." Clinch defended.

"The only thing that can save Major Dade's command is if he has disobeyed your orders, sir. As hostile as the country is through here--" He targeted his finger at the map. "--chances are he'll never reach you. I've just traveled through some of it. As we approached Micanopy, my men dismounted and charged into the swamp. We killed a few."

"General," General Clinch said with a calm demeanor, "I've shaken hands with the Indian leaders. I've danced myself into exhaustion around their campfire. I've requested rations for their starving families and understood their need to gather their crops and prepare for their journey. They're children of the forest, and it's not natural for them to want to leave the birthplace of their children or the graves of their departed. The Seminoles are suspicious of the white man and uncertain of the unknown."

"Your 'children of the forest' are out there killing innocent white folk and destroying everything the settlers have worked hard for. My men have signed up for a short-term duty. We don't have much time before they'll be returning to their families," General Call replied. "There is no time to waste. Some of them brought their own horses and supplies. They're ready for action. It is my opinion, sir, we need to move as quickly as possible and accomplish our objective expeditiously."

"Don't misunderstand me General. Since autumn, I've been convinced the war would come. There are those Indians willing to honor the treaty. However, I'm not naïve. There are also Indians determined to stay. I know they've already gathered forces and are making plans. We must not forget it's our duty to protect the farmers and pioneer families. It's in my opinion, sir, that we need a few days to prepare," General Clinch advised.

Some Indian guides came into the fort and reported, "We've found the village where the women gather food and feed the warriors, where their children hunt in the swamp, and where the men rest after attacking the whites."

"Where is it located?" General Clinch asked as he opened the map and pointed. "This is where we are, and here's the river."

One of the scouts answered, "It's located on the south side of the Withlacoochee, and we know a place where your men can cross safely."

"Ah, this is our chance. We must attack now and surprise them," General Call commanded. "I suggest, General, we travel light and go by foot to get there quickly. My men are efficient in carrying what they need on their backs. I suggest your men do the same. Leave your wagons and baggage trains here. We need to catch them off guard. Besides, my men only have a few more days before their time of service expires."

General Clinch stated, "I understand time is a factor General, but we can't leave without adequate provisions and ammunition for the men. I've ordered wagons and a baggage train to carry whatever we need."

The generals' strategies were as different as their personalities, sound of their voices, and opinions about the Seminoles. They did agree to move out and head south, but they had no idea of the murders at Fort King or the Dade massacre. Their wait for Major Dade and his men was for naught. They never came because the troops lay dead in the grass of the pine barren a long side their empty ammunition boxes.

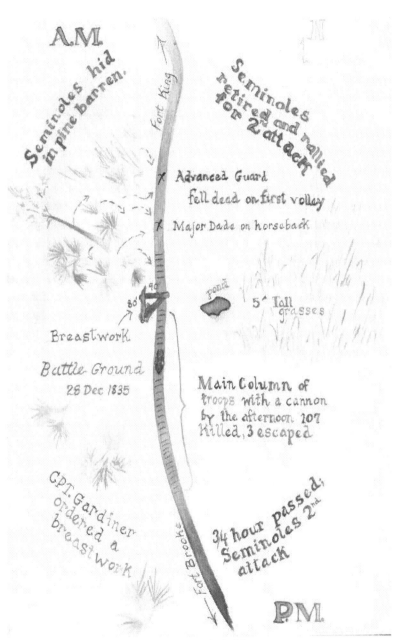

Dade's Battlefield

Chapter 10

A bizarre fog engulfed the river. Johnny and Oscee were still asleep on the bottom of the canoe, while Pop paddled the Withlacoochee alone. The black coffee-colored water melted into the shadows of the cypress trees. Pop could not see ahead of them, but heard the water rush furiously against the canoe. The current was stronger and swifter due to heavy rains.

Heavy rains. It was a dry spring, Pop thought to himself. *Why is the current so strong?*

He pulled the paddle out of the river and the current carried them further north. There was nothing he could do but let the swollen water take them.

Johnny stirred and rubbed his eyes. "Pop, where are we?"

Oscee whimpered, and Johnny patted the dog, "It's okay boy."

He grabbed the sides of the canoe. "I can barely see you, Pop."

"I'm here, son."

"Why is it so cold?" Johnny wrapped his arms tightly around Oscee to warm himself.

"I don't know, son," Pop said, calm but concerned. "The river is swelling as if we had a heavy rain. The current is carrying us toward something. All of a sudden we ran into fog, and it's thicker than pea soup."

"Where is Mr. Emil?" Johnny shivered.

"I can't see the bank. If Mr. Emil is on the bank waiting for us, he'll hear us," Pop answered.

"Pop, do you hear that?" Johnny asked. "Hear it? Men are shouting."

"Maybe it's more boatmen cleaning the river of hyacinth," Pop suggested.

"Why are they yelling? Is something wrong?" Johnny asked, "Can we get closer?"

The river had changed. There were no hyacinths on the water. The temperature dropped thirty degrees. The river had swollen due to heavy rains in the spring of that year. The current carried the canoe closer when they bumped into the bank. Pop tied the canoe to a low hanging branch.

"Pop," Johnny whispered, "what are those men doing just up ahead?"

Johnny recognized the figures of several men paddling frantically against the current from one opposite bank to another.

"Hello!" Pop called into the fog.

"Hell-o-o-o-o-o!" Someone answered back.

"Hello! Is that you Emil?" Pop called out again.

"Hell-o-o-o-o-o! Is that you Emil?"

It was his echo.

"Echo--a damn echo," Pop whispered.

The canoe started rocking back and forth.

"Johnny sit down," He said sternly.

"I am," Johnny cried. "It's not me, and it's not Oscee."

Oscee growled.

Pop reached for his son's hand. "I'm right here, son."

The canoe rocked back and forth again as the current swung the canoe closer to the bank.

Thud.

"Ah wo-o-o-o!" A howl rolled through the fog.

"What's that?" Johnny whispered. "Wolf?"

"There are no wolves around here anymore," Pop answered.

"Ah wo-o-o-o!" Something howled again.

Johnny glimpsed a flash of a white feather behind a tree. "Osceola." He whispered, "Are they here...the Seminoles?"

The sound of axe whacked trees, whoops and hollers, and voices in a different language filtered through the fog. Pop could not explain the sounds; the shouting, or the gunfire.

Johnny squinted, "What's out there?"

***

The Seminoles were ready for another battle. They watched and waited to attack more enemy soldiers. Generals Clinch and Call had left Fort Drane with the regular and volunteer armies and their Indian guides. They marched slowly and thunderously through the thick palmettos. The Seminoles knew they were coming.

"How do you expect to surprise the Indians with this heavy baggage train?" General Call criticized. "And these howling dogs your men insist on bringing will alert the Seminoles from miles away."

"Or just maybe they'll flush out the Indians," a regular defended.

"You mean flush out squirrels is all," a volunteer jeered.

The men marched by twos through the narrow passageways in the palmetto shrub. The ground became soggy with each southbound step toward the swamp.

Splash! Splunk!

The heavy wagon wheels sank into the black mud.

"Come on, men. Get a dozen of you."

"Find a log for a lever."

"Heave ho!"

The men panted and grunted as they pulled and pushed the wagons out of the soft wet bog. Their boots squished with each step as they marched, and mud caked on their thin wool trousers. They covered a few miles on dry ground and then came to another area of soggy earth. Again, wagons and animals were pulled out of the mud.

General Call grew impatient with their cumbersome movement. He thought to himself, "*This wouldn't have happened had Clinch taken my advice and left the wagons behind. There is no chance for surprise.*"

Trudging through the mud made their journey more tiring. They only covered twelve miles that day.

General Clinch commanded, "We'll camp here for the night."

"Sergeant, send a detachment to get fresh water. Watch each other's backs," a captain commanded.

"My volunteers can help," General Call offered. "After all, my Florida boys are more comfortable with this country."

There was no denying that. A few Yankees waded out in a pond to find some clean drinking water. An alligator startled the strangers when he splashed and turned his body away from them. The men dropped their pails and made huge knee-high strides out of the water to the bank. The southern boys on the bank roared with laughter.

"Those gators ain't goin' to git ya," they jeered.

"You should've seen your faces."

"They're more'n scared of ya'll."

One Yankee soldier, still shaken from his alligator encounter, said, "Well, I guess there will be no coffee tonight."

"I'll get some," a volunteer offered. "The gators are sluggish this time of year anyway. They're cold-blooded ya' know."

As he parted the reeds, a water moccasin slithered past him. "Go on, git!"

"How you gonna fight injuns if ya'll scared of gators?" a militiaman jeered.

"I've seen plenty o' fightin' in my day, lad; don' ya worry 'bout me!" another soldier replied.

Men from all nationalities and parts of the country bivouacked together that night. Campfires dried the wet soldiers while they ate. They had enough water to boil their coffee grounds and drank from tin cups. The glowing cinders danced above the fire and then vanished into the cool night air. By the next night, some of the men complained to their guide.

"Why haven't we seen them? Are they out here?"

A Negro guide told them, "Wait, Massas. You'll see; you've not walked for nothin'."

Not far away, hidden in the swamp, voices whispered around another fire. The chiefs called a council because the swamp, slough and palmetto paths brought important news. The red men sat quietly and passed around a bowl of honey water. They each took a drink of it from a ladle. Once they had shared from it, the messenger stood up. His waist belt caught the light from the fire when he spoke.

"General Clinch left Fort Drane with two hundred regulars and four hundred Florida volunteers. They've advanced into our land and are camped near the river."

The wary Chief Micanopy spoke. "We need to keep away from large forces."

However, after the night of celebration over their prior victories, the warriors were filled with confidence.

"We've no use for your faint heart," Jumper responded.

One hundred and fifty Seminoles and fifty Negros agreed. They chose to go with Osceola and Alligator.

Osceola encouraged them. "We know the swamps; they don't. You two keep watch and report their every move to us."

Osceola had commanded two young scout warriors to remain behind and watch the soldiers. They laid low in the hammock, waiting and kept a look out for the coves' invaders. The scouts entertained themselves with the movements of the white men making their way through the swamp, laughing and mocking the soldiers they had spied upon.

"Soldier fall in the mud," a jovial Seminole snickered. He imitated the white man flapping his arms and stomped his legs with a wide gait.

"He cries like a child," another warrior mimicked the soldiers.

After another day of marching, the generals' order *no campfires tonight* was passed down through the companies of men. They ate dried pork and biscuits for supper. Each felt lonely, possibly due to the uncertainty tomorrow would bring. The Florida sunshine had warmed them almost all day, but the evening air chilled them to the bone with no fire to heat their frigid bodies. The men made their beds on the hammock floor beneath a huge silver moon. They lay awake, expecting an attack from the Seminoles. Restless, they listened to sounds of Florida's wild wood--howls of red wolves, eerie hoots of small screech owls, raspy roars of panthers, deep bellows of alligators and the night trill of the whippoorwill perched above their heads. Some even wondered if what they heard was indeed nature's sounds or the signaled calls of their enemy.

The next morning at three o'clock, December thirty-first, 1835, General Clinch walked through his camp and woke Lieutenant Dancy.

"Get about forty of your men together to guard the baggage."

"Men," he called to the picket guards, "come in and prepare for the day." As he walked the frost-covered ground, men woke and others stirred. Some had never slept.

"Good morning, sir," whispered one soldier to the next.

Their breaths formed a silver vapor that glowed in the moonlight. An eager volunteer bugler forgot the order of silence and blew Reveille, even though most of the men were up.

A soldier close by grabbed his horn. "What are you doin'? Do you want the Injuns to hear us?"

General Call was disappointed to discover the man was one of his. "Man have you lost your senses? If there was any chance of surprise, we just lost it."

The young bugler hung his head in shame. "I'm sorry, sir."

He wrapped his horn, placed it in his haversack, and stood in formation with the others.

Two hours later, the command, was given. General Clinch ordered, "Forward move!"

"Forward move!" passed the lips of each officer to his next in command until every ear heard and every foot stepped forward into the cold darkness. Lieutenant Dancy remained with the small detachment guarding the baggage train and the soldiers' dogs. As the troops marched passed, they spoke firmly:

"Quiet."

"Stay."

"Hush."

"Lay."

"Shut up."

"Stop!"

The dogs watched their masters march off without them. Every muscle in their bodies quivered and quaked. They could not stay in obedience one more second. Eager to follow their masters, the pack of canines ran off, barking and howling.

"Hey, come back here!" shouted Lieutenant Dancy. He whistled in effort to call them back.

The column of men had not gone far when they heard their loyal dogs thrashing through the palmettos. The four-legged troops had no idea of the danger--or maybe they did, and that was why they followed.

General Call yelled, "You can't tell me the Indians don't know we're coming, now!"

General Clinch remained calm. A smile parted his lips, and he said, "We should have such loyalty, sir."

MURIEL TUTTLE EDEN-PAUL

Chapter 11

The howling in the nearby woods reverberated over the river. Oscee's ears perked up as he listened to the barking. He pushed his body up with his front paws, as the robust four-legged roustabouts sent their signals through the cove. Oscee growled a low gruff then in full stance in the canoe, he barked back into the night.

"It's okay boy," Johnny rubbed Oscee's chest. "We hear it too. Shh…"

The distant barking subsided and General Clinch halted his command a couple of hours later when a scout returned with his report from the river.

"Ford, too deep, too wide. Water swift," the scout reported.

"What? You assured me you knew where to cross," General Clinch whispered hoarsely. "Have you deceived me?"

Johnny reached behind him and grabbed Pop's arm. Oscee whined and sunk his head underneath the seat. The swollen river carried the travelers in their red wooden canoe to a place on the Withlacoochee River before Florida's statehood and water hyacinths--a time before steamboats brought hunting parties to shoot snowy egrets and cranes for women's fancy hats. An instance when the river was wild with sounds of red wolf, golden-eyed panther, black bear, and Seminoles, whose village was hidden deep in the cypress swamp.

In the meantime, Seminoles waited further up the river. They had planned another ambush for the soldiers. The warriors whispered behind trees and palmettos to each other.

"We've been watching for them. Where are they?"

"Can't miss them. So loud." The warriors chuckled with amusement.

"They leave a cloud of smoke from the wagons."

"Does paleface think we can't see their trail?"

"We smell their fires at night."

"Smoke too big." Laughter from the warriors rose behind their hiding places.

"Enough," said Osceola. His black steady eyes quickly commanded respect from the men. He wore a United States Army coat and white crane's plume in his hair. "Go, find them so we can fight like men. We will leave their bodies to bake in the sun. We will leave them for the vultures just like the others."

The group of men obeyed. They ran with swift feet of deer and quiet steps of the panther in search of the soldiers.

At sunrise, two and half miles away, General Clinch inspected the crossing. He thought, *If we wait and look for another crossing, we will lose more time.*

Just then he noticed an old canoe on the opposite bank and smiled. *God provides.*

"I'll go, sir," said an undressed private as he dove into the river with no fear of Seminoles, alligators, water moccasins, or the swift current.

"Stop. I didn't..." General Clinch began to say.

"It's okay, sir. He's a strong swimmer," a Lieutenant assured him.

The men cheered as he paddled and bailed the canoe back across. The General saluted the young private for his gallant effort and brave deed.

"I've made my decision," General Clinch announced. "We'll use the canoe to cross the river. Lieutenant, assign two paddlers, five men and their weapons. We'll ferry the river back and forth until everyone is across."

"Yes, sir," the young lieutenant carried out his commander's order.

It was not long before the men began their shuttle across the river. Once on the opposite bank, the soldiers got out, stacked their weapons, and waited. When the men's arms became fatigued; other men took their turn as paddlers at the bow and stern. For hours, the canoe went back and forth, carrying about six to eight men at a time. Bravely, the men ferried the river in the abandoned canoe.

General Clinch watched and encouraged the men from the bank. "Just think men, in a matter of hours, our mission will be met. We'll return victorious. We can do this. We're invincible."

"Sir, we've seen the enemies' foot prints in mud," a scout reported.

This information made General Clinch more determined.

It took all morning for over two hundred soldiers and twenty-seven volunteers to reach the southern bank.

One of the volunteers, Dill, said to a man in the canoe. "Take my musket and powder. I didn't come all this way for nothin'. I ain't goin' to miss a good fight." Then he jumped on his horse as it swam across.

General Clinch cheered, "That is what I like to see another brave man going into battle. Good Job, Dill!"

Twenty-six other men followed, some on horseback while others swam or floated across on logs.

In the meantime, Seminole scouts returned to tell Osceola the white men were crossing the river at a different spot than they expected. Osceola decided he would move his men further south and wait for the tired soldiers to stack their weapons and rest in the cleared area. The Seminoles had painted their bodies for battle. Half their faces and necks were painted a bright pigment of red-orange and streaked with black. They lay hidden behind grass, palmetto shrubs, and trees. A feather flashed behind a tree as they peered to look at the activity.

Osceola spoke, "We'll wait until the river divides them."

"They're not many, we can overcome them," Alligator assured.

The chiefs watched and remained ready for the right moment.

General Call shouted, "General, there's a piece of land jutting out into the river."

Then General Clinch ordered his men, "Get your men to put logs onto it. We'll bridge the rest."

"Indians!" Men's voices echoed the warning. "Indians are coming!"

"Men, face the forest. Keep your backs to the river!" General Call shouted to the rest of his volunteers on the north side of the river.

A few men shot before orders were given.

Zap!

Zing!

They fired, not knowing where the Seminoles hid. Sounds of the wild wood came alive with the resonance of the warrior. Seminole war shrills made the bravest soldier shiver. Grabbing their guns the soldiers formed a line of battle and fired.

"Whaaaaaooooop!"

Osceola gestured his warriors to fire and advance behind the trees and palmettos.

Whap!

Thud.

A soldier fell.

Meanwhile, the men on the south side of the river frantically ran for their weapons.

General Clinch ran for his horse, shouting orders, "Two lines, men. Form two battle lines. Fire. Don't stop! Keep Firing."

Rapid fire and smoke rose from the clearing and surrounded the palmettos.

Lieutenant Colonel Fanning shouted, "Get your bayonets men. *Charge!*"

The center artillery companies fell back against endless volleys of the enemies' bullets.

General Clinch rode his horse into the stunned soldiers. "Get up, men," he yelled. "Extend and charge the enemy!"

They surprised the Seminoles with their advance into the shrub and swamp. Another order was given. "Companies to the rear, *charge!*"

Someone shouted, "They're moving forward on the right."

"On the left flank, sir."

General Clinch rode his horse back across the lines to the left. "Charge! Drive them back! Don't let them advance!"

He stayed with his men and was an inspiration to each fighting spirit. A bullet sped from the hammock and hit him in the sleeve. Another ball put a hole through his cap and singed his hair. He sat calm in his saddle and said, "I do believe those fellows are firing at me." Then he dismounted from his horse, walked among the men and commanded, *"Charge!"*

In the hammock, Osceola led his men bravely into battle with shrill calls and flails of his arms. He stepped from behind a tree, aimed, and fired. His bullets hit his enemy with accuracy. He encouraged his warriors to advance and kept shooting his weapon even with a wounded arm.

A soldier yelled, "Retreat!" and the troops began to run.

General Clinch's resolve under enemy fire pressed on. "Hold the line!" He encouraged his men, "I'm ready to die on the spot if necessary, but not retreat."

Some soldiers continued to run.

"And if you choose to retreat, I'll shoot any man who does," he threatened.

He shouted again, "Charge! One more time. Drive them back. Hold your position men!"

After seventy minutes of fighting, worn out troops were relieved when they heard "The savages are retreating." They waited until they were sure there was no more enemy gunfire.

General Call crossed the river, but most of his volunteers remained on the north bank protecting the road back to Fort Drane. He found the general fatigued from the fight.

"You were right," he admitted. "I thought I saw Tiger Tail among them."

"It wouldn't surprise me if you did, General. The Seminoles have learned to fit in and conduct themselves according to our expectations, especially if it benefits their cause." The weary Clinch added, "We didn't find their hideout, and I've underestimated the Seminole's ability to fight. Neither of us won."

"No, General, but you held them. Maybe we shouldn't ask more than that," General Call said. "The militia's service is almost over, so it's my recommendation we don't pursue the enemy into the swamp."

"General, I'd appreciate your supervision getting the men back across. Tie the canoe up to the logs, and then we'll walk the men back," Clinch replied.

Then he turned to one of his officers, "Captain, assign your men to get the wounded and bring the dead with you."

Some soldiers walked into the palmettos looking for bodies. "I'm gonna git me a savage scalp to prove I did battle," one man boasted.

"Why do you need to prove anything?" another soldier asked with disdain. "We've enough to do to get the wounded across the river."

The smoke still lingered in the swamp underneath the cypress and stately oaks. Seminole and Army bullets were lodged in tree trunks, sheared palm fronds, killed, and wounded men. General Clinch and General Call returned to Fort Drane.

Osceola and Alligator returned to their village with their warriors, confident their swamp hideout was still a mystery to the white man. Osceola's son waited for his father until he returned with a wounded arm after the battle. The medicine man, Abiaka, made a poultice from the crushed inner bark of oak. Before he applied it to Osceola's arm, he blew on his herbal dressing to empower it with the healing spirits. With his wound healed, Osceola rested and would return to the next battle in the cove a few months later.

Johnny, Pop and Oscee looked for the take out point, calling for Mr. Emil in the gray light of dusk. The fog lifted but twilight felt cool against Johnny's sunburn. He shivered, sandwiched in between the past and present. He squinted toward the bank and made out a man's silhouette standing there.

"Mr. Emil is that you?" He called. "Pop, I see someone standing on the edge. I can't tell if it is a soldier, Seminole, or Mr. Emil."

No one answered from the darkness. All they heard was the sound of water lapping against the canoe and grumbling stomachs.

"I'm hungry. Is there anything to eat?"

"No, son, it's all gone," Pop told him. "Don't worry. I am sure we'll find Mr. Emil soon."

"I smell something good," Johnny sniffed the air. "Do you smell that?"

Oscee sat up and held his nose in the air, and his nostrils quivered from the scent of food.

Maybe we are close to the Seminoles' village? Maybe Osceola's wife cooked a rabbit over the fire, or maybe it was a fish her son caught in the river to feed the great chief. Johnny thought. Whatever it was, the aroma made him hungry.

"We'll paddle closer to the bank and see if there is something we can see." said Pop.

MURIEL TUTTLE EDEN-PAUL

Chapter 12

It was New Year's Day, 1836, and the smell of pork and beans wafted over the woods near Fort Drane. General Clinch ladled the bubbling beans from a black iron cauldron onto his tin plate. He ate the hot meal with his troops within the safety of Fort Drane. Afterward, he made his rounds, visiting the sick and wounded who lay on the earth floor. A loyal and faithful dog lay next to the feverish body of his master. He licked his wounds and never left his side. The soldier lifted his gun-powdered fingers to pat the muzzle of his companion.

General Clinch knelt at his side. "My poor man," he whispered. "Bear your sufferings as a soldier, as you must now become a soldier of Christ. Put your trust in Him. He is your commander and your salvation."

His words not only encouraged the dying soldier but encouragement for himself. He had just received the tragic news of Dade's massacre.

Once the news reached Washington, it traveled across the rest of the country by express riders. News reports sparked many a young man's patriotic spirit and a quixotic quest for the Florida wilderness, especially in the southern boys. The settlers and plantation owners who lived in the tropical territory panicked and fled to neighboring forts for protection. No one was safe.

Express riders on horseback brought the news to the commander of the Western Department, General Edmund Pendleton Gaines in New Orleans, Louisiana. He received the official report verifying the gruesome details about the horrific deaths of his brothers in arms. His passion ignited action. He immediately wrote a letter to Washington urging the War Department to move quickly into the frontier. He wrote another letter to the Governor of Louisiana requesting volunteers to aid this serious emergency. Thankfully, there was no shortage of citizen soldiers who rallied to the cause.

"Lieutenant McCall, I'm glad you've arrived from Memphis in time to accompany me," General Gaines greeted. "I'm surprised I've not yet heard from Washington. The severity of the situation can no longer wait for the poor express riders to reach me. It's my duty as an officer to go forth rapidly. I'll not wait any longer for official orders but will act upon my belief this is the right thing to do. Beside, my military record in the War of 1812 qualifies me to act thus. At least the Governor of Louisiana has understood the severity."

"Yes, sir," Lieutenant McCall saluted the general. "It's a pleasure to serve with you."

On a cool February morning in New Orleans, 1836, the Reveille bugle roused troops to rise up.

"The regiment of volunteers under the command of Colonel Persifer F. Smith have embarked with part of the Fourth Infantry in a brig," Lieutenant McCall reported. "And two companies of artillery armed as infantry are aboard the little steamer, Florida. They're ready for your inspection."

Immediately, Gaines inspected the troops on board. "The Governor of Louisiana has promptly supplied me with fine men for my campaign. This yeomanry of the south has exchanged hoes for muskets prudently defending our country against this invading foe."

Gaines saluted Colonel Persifer F. Smith. "Sir, I put these men in your command."

The general and his staff boarded the Florida and set sail for Pensacola. "We'll stop in Pensacola for supplies of wood, water, and fresh provisions," commanded General Gaines. "Lieutenant, inform the troops."

The steamboat's wheel churned the water in motion. The boat was heavily loaded with a dozen horses and about eleven hundred men headed for Fort Brooke.

"Excuse me, sir," a messenger interrupted. "I was delayed to get this message to you. I barely made your departure."

"What do *you* want?" Gaines retorted. "I'm not turning around. I guess you won't mind traveling to Pensacola."

"This letter came for you from Adjutant-General Albert Jones." The messenger handed him an envelope.

General Gaines broke the seal. "Are these my orders? You're dismissed."

He read out loud, "General Gaines, You are to remain in New Orleans." Then he interjected gruffly, "A little late for that." He continued, "Please find enclosed a copy of your orders: 'Order No. 7', which from Secretary Cass. Signed Adjutant-General Albert Jones."

What should I do? He thought. *The Seminoles have refused relocation, which requires my immediate attention. If we act now we have a chance, no time should be lost. If we wait too long, I'll miss my chance.*

He looked into an empty envelope, with a self-satisfied smile, he said, "Lieutenant, look in this envelope and tell me what you see."

"Nothing, sir. It appears 'Order No. 7' is missing." Lieutenant McCall confirmed.

"Have I not promised the volunteers their wages? Have I not responded out of duty and honor? Am I not a man of my word?" He asked.

"Most certainly, sir."

General Gaines face furrowed in a scowl, indignant he said, "I will NOT take orders from Adjutant-General Jones, an inferior officer. He doesn't have the ability to perform sound judgment for me. Besides, I'm not holding 'official orders' which I could disobey. Please call the commanders of my troops so we can discuss this matter."

The other commanders gathered and awaited General Gaines's orders. Once he discussed the situation with them, they responded with support and encouragement to proceed south to Fort Brooke as planned.

Colonel Smith said, "Sir, the volunteers are unwilling to proceed without you. My men respect you. We're ready for a good fight."

"As far as we know, Indian-Negroes have hemmed in Fort Brooke. I don't have any other choice but to proceed as planned. Thank you, gentlemen.," Gaines concluded. He was determined to get to Fort Brooke and remain in the field until advised otherwise from the War Department. At that time, General Gaines had no knowledge that General Scott had been assigned to the Florida territory instead of him.

They arrived at Fort Brook on February fourth and found the fort barren of expected supplies. The commanding officer reported that there had been no news from General Clinch. They had no idea if the enemy had attacked again. General Gaines also learned the dismal news that another settlement had been burned and plundered. Most of the settlers had been murdered, but a few escaped to the fort for protection. These events happened more frequently, so General Gaines gathered his commanding officers together.

He walked back and forth in front of them with his hands behind his back. "Men, we need to surprise these Indian-Negroes from their hiding place in the Cove. We don't have adequate provisions for the troops. If we disregard our principles, we'll expose another body of troops to another disaster. Based on the principles of military law, it's our duty to spare the populace of the tomahawk and knife."

The officers concurred.

"Now, we must ask ourselves, what might we get along without and what might we need on our march. The quartermaster can't supply us with enough provisions based on the amount of families who have come to the fort for protection."

"Sir," said Lieutenant McCall, "the quartermaster has been able to procure another dozen horses and ten days of rations for the troops. Five of which they'll carry in their haversack."

"Fine, lieutenant. I trust you'll divide them up between the commanding officers and use the rest as packhorses. We leave in the morning."

The next morning, February thirteenth, the troops set out at daybreak beneath the shelter of sprawling oak tree branches. The pioneer women in the fort brought food they had prepared and wished them luck. Each captain formed his company behind him. General Gaines was pleased with the self-denial and self-sacrifice he witnessed in the men. They paraded with confidence through dense palmettos, prepared to battle the Seminoles, pulling a cannon and carrying their weapons. Upon his horse, General Gaines led the column of men and horses, while friendly Indians guided them through the unknown wilderness.

Lieutenant McCall rode behind General Gaines. *He is a true soldier,* he thought. *Willing to share in hardships, dangers, and deprivations with all of us.*

The men knew it, too. They marched north on a narrow trail through the palmettos along the east bank of the river--the same trail Major Dade and his men marched a few months before. The men spread out along the trail, and palmettos crackled as their bodies pushed through the dense scrub. Warblers wintering in the southernwoods scolded their footsteps. They did not see or hear one Seminole.

On the eighth day, the murmurs of their voices fell into silence when they came upon the open field and found the bodies of Dade and his men. Vultures lurked in nearby trees. The soldiers stared, motionless but still breathing, upon a field of men who had no breath left at all. The pinewoods whispered the grim news as musket balls still pierced their bark. The spiked grass cradled the dead men when bullets stopped their last breath.

General Gaines got off his horse and broke the silence. "Station a guard around the perimeter. The rest of you have permission to walk the battlefield. Try to identify anyone you can. We'll pick a burial place and dig two trenches; one for the officers, and one for militia and regular soldiers who fought bravely side by side."

"General," said Lieutenant McCall, "the bodies strewn about appear as if a child had tired of playing with tin toy soldiers."

"But they aren't toy soldiers are they?" General Gaines replied. "They're men with grieving widows, sons and daughters, mothers and fathers, and…a country."

Cautiously, regular and volunteer troops stepped around bodies. The men spoke in hushed voices when they found someone they knew. Major Dade's body was found at the edge of the field. A bullet had pierced his chest. His body was stripped of his coat and shirt, but his hair and beard remained. Even though his flesh had shrunk, Lieutenant McCall recognized the brave major who fell in battle leading his men. Then he walked into the triangular breastwork and examined the men within it. Some men's heads lay upon the breastwork as they were shot in the forehead.

He said, "Their bodies are still kneeling or extending in a shooting position. Sir, I recognize Gardiner in the center. I remember him from West Point."

Other soldiers took somber steps in between bodies fallen over logs or in dry grass. A few bodies had been stabbed. For a moment- -a brief moment--they hoped their brothers in arms would once again stretch to life and join them in battle. Reality stunned them, as life would not be restored to the fallen. However, God gave courage to the living soldiers who stumbled upon the massacre; they carefully buried their dead comrades side by side in trenches. They found a cannon ball, a six pounder, in a nearby pond, which they placed on a grave.

General Gaines commanded, "Get your men back into your

columns."

Each captain formed his company behind him. The Fourth Regiment band marched at the head of the column leading the funeral parade of drums, fife, and bugles, which replaced the sounds of Withlacoochee's wildlife. The music serenaded their sorrowed hearts. They reversed their arms and slowly paraded around the field.

General Gaines whispered, "I've never witnessed a nobler sight of self-devotion and self-sacrifice in all my years as a soldier, or perhaps throughout our history."

No one spoke as the mournful notes wept; a breeze whispered the men's names to heaven. The column of men marched around the bloodstained field as tears fell from their faces and flowed like the current of the Withlacoochee River.

Chapter 13

"Pop, I can't reach it," Johnny said.

The current had pulled the rope taut, and the knot was beyond his reach.

"I'll pull us closer to the branch and give the rope some slack." Pop grabbed the rope hand over hand, pulling the canoe against the swift current back to the branch. "The river's running fast. She wants to carry us away. Be careful, son."

Johnny stood up and rocked the canoe; he stepped forward and untied the knot. Their release gave the river permission to take them closer to another crossing.

"I'm going to paddle against the river to the other side. Mr. Emil must be waiting."

When Pop put his paddle in the water, the river grabbed it, with a mind of its own, and turned them back around. They headed north in the swift current.

"What's the matter, Pop? Why are we going this way?" Johnny asked, frightened.

He did not want to be on the river anymore. He was hungry and wanted to go home. Where was Mr. Emil? Where was the take out point?

"The river's too wide and deep here. Maybe we should go further. Mr. Emil has to be waiting for us by now," Pop reassured him.

The river current carried the red wooden canoe to another place, another battle, another time, and another X.

"Pop, do you hear that?" Johnny asked. He took a deep breath, "It's happening again."

The Indians opened fire from the shadows on the other side of the bank.

"Are they shooting at us?" Johnny cried, "Pop, I want to go home!"

"Lay down in the canoe, son."

***

After the funeral, General Gaines and his men marched on the military road toward Fort King. When the men heard the command, "Forward march!" they pushed through dense palmettos. General Gaines turned his attention toward Lieutenant McCall. "Lieutenant, this letter from the quartermaster reassures me that at least the men will be fed. I'm gratified to know a large amount of provisions has been sent from New York and will be there for us. Although I don't understand what's happened to General Clinch. I've always known him to be a man I can count on. We don't know anything about his current situation, nor do we have any knowledge of Indian movement in the cove. Our last report stated he's been stationed at Fort King since Agent Thompson's murder."

"Yes sir, supplies should be in Fort King by now," Lieutenant McCall added. "Our men have used up their rations. It helped that we were able to procure a few days worth at Alafia."

Gaines said, "It's our duty to continue, lieutenant. Our main objective is to find the Seminoles and drive them out with all the fire power we can."

"Sir, why haven't we seen any red men?" A captain complained. "The men are getting restless."

"Since we haven't met General Clinch on our march, I suspect Indians have surrounded him at Fort King. After what we just saw at Dade's battlefield, we need to be prepared for anything. Get your men ready, Captain," General Gaines remarked.

"Yes, sir."

They arrived at Fort King on February twenty-second. There were no Seminoles, no food, and no General Clinch. The Third Artillery, which commanded the fort, had sparse rations for themselves.

General Gaines said to the commanding officer, "I'm disappointed to learn Fort King is without men and supplies. Where is General Clinch? Have my reinforcements joined him?"

"No, sir," the officer continued, "General Clinch returned with his command to Fort Drane about twenty-two miles north. He still has his four artillery companies and one infantry. Two volunteer companies from the northern territory have joined him there."

General Gaines was hopeful, even though the present situation looked bleak. "Well, I can count on the citizen soldier to be sure. Sir, can you spare your rations?"

"No, sir. We barely have enough to feed our own men. It's the same at Fort Drane. Sir, I think you should know, too; General Scott is already in Picolata making plans for his campaign to take command over Florida."

"WHAT?" General Gaines angered to hear this news. "It's possible it'll take him time to get things in order. However, since there're no provisions, I'm left with no choice but to return to Fort Brooke. I'll make Tampa Bay my headquarters. Lieutenant, send another message to General Clinch and let him know my decision."

General Gaines studied the torn yellow map he unfolded from his pocket. "We'll cross the river and return on the road by Chocochatee."

"Sir," another officer interjected, pointing to an area of the cove, "you're most likely to run into Indians. We've reports they're set up in this area here."

"All the better!" Gaines recaptured his desire and ambition to succeed. "Let's proceed as planned."

His men believed in him and he was determined not to let them down. Once again, he ordered the march of one thousand men through Seminole territory to reclaim the frontier for new settlements. Some of the friendly Indian guides moved onto Fort Drane, but ten remained to help General Gaines find the ford in the river.

"Split up into three wings," General Gaines ordered. "We need to remember what our mission is. The element of surprise is crucial. We haven't seen the enemy so far, but they're out there. We know what they can do. If we split up, we can comb the area better and meet at the river. We'll cross at the ford near where Clinch fought the Indians, so be alert. Keep watch."

They arrived at the river on February twenty-seventh. A soldier reported to Gaines, "Sir, the guides can't find the ford."

"What do you mean they can't find the ford?" Gaines shouted at the soldier. "Keep looking. We're going to search until we find it. We've come this far; I'm not giving up!"

The guides and troops searched for almost an hour when it finally happened. The Indians opened fired from the shadows on the other side of the river.

"The river is too wide and deep," Gaines called. "We can't cross here. Keep firing, men."

"Sir, rifles are being fired from the left and center, but we don't see anyone," an officer reported to Gaines.

"Just keep firing. At least we know we have met the enemy," Gaines said satisfied.

The soldiers at Fort Drane could hear guns echoing through the piney woods and wondered if they were Gaines's, the Seminoles', or both. The men put their ears to the ground to hear the message of another battle on the river.

After a short time, the firing stopped. For some men, it had been their first military fight.

"The guides tell me the ford is about three miles below us. We'll look for it in the morning," Gaines told his officers. "Captain, give me your report."

"One killed and seven wounded, sir."

"Tell the men we'll camp here for the night."

The next morning, February twenty-eighth, three columns of men marched three more miles following a trail along the river.

"Lieutenant Izard, take your dragoons to the river and see if we should cross there," his captain ordered.

The young lieutenant stepped into the river, only to find again that it was too deep to cross. Before he could say anything, a single bullet struck him in the nose, and exited through his temple. He dropped to the ground and mustered wispy words, "Keep your positions, men, and lie close."

His men quickly pulled his slumped body to safety. The enemy's war whoop silenced birds' songs and announced rapid shooting of rifles. The sunlight, which had filtered through the hammock, vanished under a veil of gun smoke.

"I'm impressed with their fire power," General Gaines said and commanded his men to keep firing.

"Where are they, sir? I hear their war cries. They shoot behind wild shrubs. I don't see them. They're like ghost warriors," an officer said.

"Keep shooting," Gaines commanded. He turned his attention to an officer next to him and shouted, "Get your men; build a pontoon bridge. We're going to cross this river!"

"Yes, sir! Get your axes men! Chop some pine! We'll bridge across this river," the captain ordered.

Later in the afternoon, more war whoops echoed through the cove. Micanopy showed up with almost eight hundred warriors. The troops heard a thrashing of palmetto as the warriors reached the other side of Withlacoochee.

"Captain, we need to fortify our position. Start building a breastwork, and get Lieutenant Izard and any other wounded

inside," General Gaines commanded.
   "Yes, sir."

CAMP IZARD

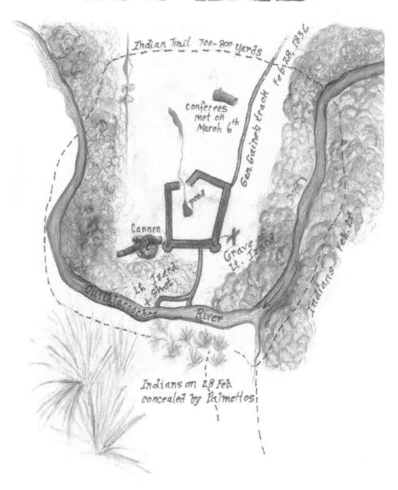

The gunfire ceased by evening. The men took some comfort in

the quiet behind their breastwork, built about three feet tall from pine logs. Leaning against the logs, General Gaines penned a letter:

Dear General Clinch,

We have been fired upon relentlessly this day, February 28th. This afternoon, more warriors have joined our enemy in the shrub. I am quite sure the whole force of them has surrounded us. I urge you, sir, to come at once with mounted men. I suggest you cross the river higher up, move down on the left bank, and attack from the rear. It is my desire and yours that we bring an end to this war while we have the chance. Please bring ample supply of ammunition and provisions. I will continue to amuse the Indians and prepare my boats for crossing, but I will not do so until I hear from you."

~ E.P.Gaines

"Lieutenant, find a runner of great speed and agility to take this message to Fort Drane," Gaines said. "See that Clinch gets it."

Lieutenant Izard lay still as one of his men gently lifted his lips to a bottle of whiskey, which he had tucked into his haversack.

"This might help, sir. We named our new fort after you--Camp Izard."

The dying soldier parted his lips into a faint smile.

During the night, the men listened to the hoot of a barred owl perched in a tall pine.

Whoooo cooooks for youuuu? Whoooo cooooks for youuuu?

A Louisiana volunteer listened to its rhythmic song and thought, *Who cooks for me?* He answered, "My wife cooks for me. She's probably cooking venison on the hearth back home. I'll be home soon to a warm meal." Such a thought comforted him. His stomach grumbled as he tried to sleep in the wild woods, but the sounds and smells of the night made him and the others restless.

The following morning, about ten o'clock on February twenty-ninth, the men awoke to bullets coming into Camp Izard from three directions. The men leapt into action and started shouting at one another.

"Get your men out into the scrub."

"Yes, sir."

"You men stay inside and secure the fort."

"The Red Sticks are advancing!"

"Watch out! Heavy fire coming from the north!"

"Keep shooting!"

"Do you see them?"

"That man is wounded. Pull him in; I'll cover you."

"Sir, one man has been killed and seven wounded," Lieutenant McCall reported to Gaines, who shouted confidently over the gunfire.

"We've got them now!"

Just at that moment, the Seminoles crept unnoticed close to the breastwork and lit a fire. The men saw the flames swiftly coming towards them; smoked burned their eyes.

"They lit a grass fire. Those savages are tryin' to burn us out," a soldier yelled.

"Scrub's on fire!" another man yelled.

"I see them, sir. They're advancing," cried a volunteer.

"Sir, the flames are rolling towards us," announced a soldier, who had perched his gun on the pine logs.

"The wind shifted," another soldier proclaimed.

"Fire! Keep firing!"

The Louisiana volunteers guarded their position in Camp Izard, and their attackers were killed.

"Lieutenant, the whole strength of warriors is upon us," Gaines shouted. "Run a message up to Colonel Foster on the front."

Lieutenant McCall delivered the message to the north front and returned to General Gaines unharmed.

The general said in a slow and steady voice, "I'm glad to see, sir, that you have a very good stomach for war."

Lieutenant McCall's facial expression went from smile to shock when a rifle ball struck General Gaines. The general's head whipped back. He uttered a low grunt, leaned forward, and blood dripped from his mouth.

Lieutenant McCall asked, "General, are you badly hurt?"

"No," General Gaines replied. He reached into his mouth and said, "Here is the ball." His teeth had left an indent on it. He wiped his mouth on his sleeve and said, "It's mean of the redskins to knock out my teeth when I have so few."

The firing on both sides continued until the middle of the night. The wildlife had escaped to safer parts of the woods. That night, the owl would not hunt, nor the red wolf. The panther kept his distance. Insects did not hum; nor did frogs croak from the muddy banks. After midnight, the last shot was fired, and the troops rested safely inside the breastwork. The Seminoles fought forcefully. The warriors felt they had fought 'as they had never fought before'. Some crossed back over the river to sleep in the shrub, and others went back to their families in the swamp. An eerie cloak of silence fell upon the darkness except for a small flame from the general's candle. He leaned his back against a log and wrote to General Clinch.

February 29
General Clinch,

My troops fired with coolness and precision today under the constant force of the Indian fighter. I much admire his gallantry and have never seen such fighting. I now believe a direct movement would be best instead of crossing higher up as I suggested yesterday. I am convinced you should bring your mounted men as the Indians move with much quickness and agility. I shall not move into enemy territory until I hear from you. I urge you to come as soon as possible, while we have the chance.

~ E.P. Gaines

The following day, it seemed as though the Seminoles were at rest, except for casual gunfire. The random shots were a reminder

Seminoles were still there, close by to be certain. They watched the troops' movements and fired when someone left camp. On the morning of March second, General Gaines and his men were again under fire in Camp Izard.

"We've got them now, men. We can hold them until General Clinch gets here," Gaines encouraged the troops.

Where is Clinch? He is usually very prompt, Gaines thought.

He did not want to discourage the hope his men had as they all looked forward to the sound of horses crashing through the palmettos.

Any minute, they thought.

However, they knew it still could be days before anyone came. General Gaines inspected his troops, who were tired, thin, and starved. What more could he expect of them? They had given so much. They would have to ration what little food was left in their haversacks.

"Men, whatever corn you still have left, turn it in, and it'll be divided equally among you," the quartermaster announced. "General Gaines decided we must butcher some horses. We don't know when General Clinch will arrive."

The men agreed to eat horsemeat to feed their hunger and win the war.

Lieutenant Izard suffered the next five days of his life during the continued fighting. He was restless and exhausted, while his Louisianans looked after him with endearment. After his death, his men mourned the southern gentleman from whom they had learned valuable lessons. Over the next several days, enemy bullets whizzed overhead and war whoops yipped and yelled in the woods. More men were killed and wounded. The men became accustomed to the warrior's war cry, but each time they heard it, it was menacing reminder of what would follow.

Finally, March fifth, a voice called into the night.

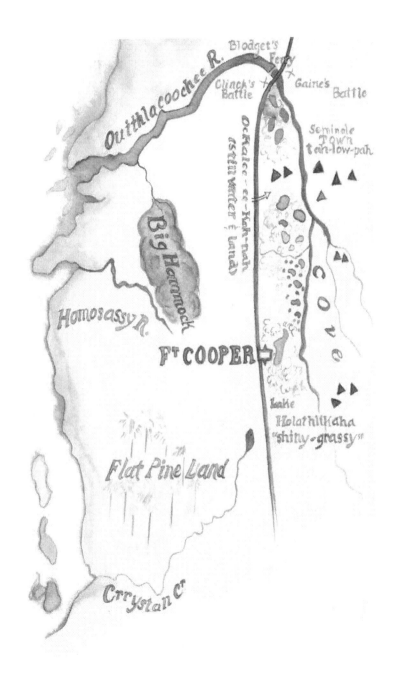

MURIEL TUTTLE EDEN-PAUL

Chapter 14

"Hello-o-o!"

"Hello," Pop answered.

"Hello!" a voice called back. "John is that you?"

"Emil! Over here!" Pop yelled.

"Mr. Emil," Johnny yelled and waved his arms back and forth. "Over here! We're over here!"

Oscee barked as Mr. Emil's truck's lights beamed over the water. Pop paddled toward the light.

"I'm sorry I'm late," Mr. Emil apologized.

"I'm surprised you made it through the fog," Pop said.

"Fog? What fog?" Mr. Emil questioned.

Johnny looked around the river. There was not one wisp of fog left behind. The sky was deep purple. The sun had set behind cypress trees and left a thin, wavy, brilliant, neon orange outline over treetops. A rush of bats flew in and out of the woods diving for mosquitoes. A barred owl hooted in a cypress tree, waking up the swamp's night creatures. The river flowed smoothly around a bounty of water hyacinth. Johnny was so happy to see Mr. Emil, he forgot how hungry and tired he was.

"Yes, *thick* fog. Fog thicker than..."

Pop gently placed his hand on his son's shoulder and patted. "Maybe we had too much sun today."

"But Pop, you know the fog was thicker than pea soup and we heard…" Johnny wanted to tell Mr. Emil all about their day.

"Son…" Pop looked down at him.

"Why don't ya'll come by and see what Miss Sadie's fixin'," Mr. Emil suggested. "Then you can tell us about your river adventure."

"Are you sure Miss Sadie won't mind?" Pop asked politely. They both were starving and would savor a home-cooked meal. "That's mighty kind of you, Emil."

"No, she'd love to have you. Come on; hop in. Oscee, you get in the back with the canoe. There's no room for you up front."

They turned into Emil's place. Scattered orange trees flanked the sandy drive. The chickens had gone to roost in their branches. As they stepped upon the front porch, old Oscar, a gray tomcat, lunged out of the darkness onto Oscee's back. The dog went wailing right underneath the porch.

Mr. Emil laughed. "Show folks some hospitality, Oscar! Sorry, John. He's mean, but a damn good mouser."

"It's alright," Pop said, chuckling at the sight.

Johnny was sympathetic, "Poor Os. He almost got eaten by a gator, and now this."

Miss Sadie came to the screen door in bare feet. She wore a cotton dress with a calico apron tied around her waist. "Emil, you brought company?" She smiled and greeted her guests. "Good. Too much for just you and me. Hey, Johnny. It's so good to see you, Hon." She gave him a big hug and kiss on the cheek. "Every time I see you, it's dark."

Miss Sadie was one of their customers. She gave Pop a hug too. "Wash up, at the pump handle," she said. "I don't have one of them fancy faucets, yet, but I've been after Mr. Emil to put one in for me."

Mr. Emil laughed, "Pump handle works fine. Here; sit down and eat!"

Miss Sadie was about the same age as Mrs. Jaeger, though a little taller and thinner. Johnny felt good sitting in her kitchen. The table was covered with a red calico tablecloth and set with white enamelware. A small, blue glass bottle filled with pink geraniums served as her centerpiece. The gas lantern cast a yellow glow across the room. The iron skillet on the cook stove steamed with a smell of goodness; fried quail in rich brown gravy. Mr. Emil tucked a napkin into his overalls. "I shot some quail this mornin', I had a feelin' ya'll might come for supper."

Johnny never thought he could be so hungry. Miss Sadie heaped his plate with grits and young quail smothered in onions and gravy. It melted in his mouth and was the best meal he had ever tasted. Yes, he might go so far to say, better than Mrs. Jaeger's German sausage and spaetzle with gravy.

"I made biscuits this morning," Miss Sadie said. "So they ain't hot, but here's some kumquat marmalade to put on 'em. It was too hot to bake this afternoon."

No one noticed the temperature of the biscuits. They sopped up the hot gravy just fine. Johnny took his biscuits and wiped his plate clean. He licked his fingers and looked up to see if anyone noticed. No one did. He felt full to the top with quail, biscuits, and gravy. He could not eat another bite...until Miss Sadie ladled peach dumpling into his bowl with a scoop of home churned vanilla ice cream. It was the richest and creamiest he had ever swirled in his mouth.

Miss Sadie teased, "John, I blame you for our extra pounds--you and your Jersey cows." She smiled, "You boys have been way too quiet. Tell us; how was your canoe trip?"

Johnny told her about the alligator, coon tracks, and the Great Blue Heron, then said, "I fell asleep and when I woke up we were in fog, and it was freezing."

"Cold? It can get cold in winter, but not this time of year," she laughed. "This has to be the hottest June on record."

Concerned, she looked at Pop, "John, maybe the boy has some heat sickness. Maybe you should let Doc take a look at him?"

"Then we heard gunfire and saw soldiers crossing the river!" Johnny wanted to tell them everything.

Miss Sadie reached over the table and felt his forehead.

"He's all right, Sadie. Don't go fussin' over the boy," Mr. Emil said. "Tell me more about the soldiers, Johnny."

He kept talking about what he had seen that day--the Seminoles, the soldiers, the battles, and their generals. He had been where the X's marked the spots on Pop's map. He had smelled the gun smoke underneath the cypress trees. He had heard men fall and horses' hooves trample through the hammock. Mr. Emil did not laugh or make fun of him. He knew from experience exactly what had happened.

"Can someone tell me what happened to General Gaines?" Johnny asked.

Mr. Emil smiled, "Clinch rescued him, much to the dismay of General Winfield Scott, who was on his way. He'd ordered Clinch not to come to Gaines's aid."

"Is that why Gaines didn't know what happened to him?" Johnny asked.

"Clinch and Gaines were friends," Pop added. "Clinch couldn't stand to hear the distant fire another minute. So he brought food from his plantation to Gaines's men. When he came upon them, he saw some Seminoles in their camp. Clinch didn't notice the white flag of peace, so he fired upon the Seminoles, who fled back into the swamp. Gaines eventually turned his troops over to Clinch because he had to leave Florida. General Scott was in command of the territory, and he had his own plan."

"What plan?" Johnny asked.

"I think we've had enough for one day, son. It's late, and we need to get home. I'm glad I asked the Bellamy boy down Moccasin Slough to milk the cows and do our chores for us. Dawn will come soon enough. Good night, Emil, Miss Sadie, and thank you."

Mr. Emil and Pop shook hands.

"Oh, I almost forgot. Thanks for shuttling my truck back over."

"My pleasure, John. Goodnight."

Johnny fell asleep in the truck on the way home. When they arrived, Oscee took his post on the front porch. Pop carried his son inside and laid him on his bed. A nice wind blew off the lake, moving stifling heat out of the house. The map still lay open on the table and moved slightly in the breeze. The winding line of the river flowed past Fort Brook, Fort Drane, Fort King, Dade's Battle, Gaines's Battle, and Clinch's Battle...

Chapter 15

Johnny had been in Florida for a month. His Jersey calf had grown and followed him in the paddock like a puppy. The sun had bleached his hair blonder and bronzed his skin. His feet were callused from running across the farm barefoot. Everyone in town knew him, and he felt like a real Florida boy. One day, he and Pop went into town for supplies. They ate lunch at the soda-fountain counter in Vann's drug store. Pop ordered two fried catfish 'blue plate specials.

"Comin' right up," the waitress said.

Pop's friend, Mr. Flint, came in and sat next to him. The men shook hands.

"Hey, Buddy, how are ya'? And your crops?" Pop asked.

Mr. Flint, a thin, grey-haired man, lifted his hat to scratch his forehead. "Purty good. I planted two fields of soybeans and corn, every other row. Thought I'd experiment this year and try some velvet beans, soy, and peanuts."

"Where did you get the peanut seed?" Pop asked.

"Found some in Ocala. I'm getting along better since I found some good farm hands a few weeks ago. Garden's all planted. Soon Bessie will be busy cannin' 'fore she teaches, come school time."

" ' got any hogs to sell?"

"No, I just sold two weighing over five hundred pounds. Got a good price too," Mr. Flint said proudly.

Johnny finished eating and got down while the men talked. Nobody could just go to town and come back. There was always someone to talk to about something. Johnny bought another postcard to send to Mother. This one had a picture of broken alligator eggs and two baby gators crawling out. He wrote:

Dear Mother,

I can drink the water without holding my nose. Sandspurs don't prick my feet. Pop and I watched a gator cross the lake when we fished. I haven't named my calf yet.

XOXO

Your Son,

Johnny

He wished she would change her mind about moving south. They could all three sit at the counter, sip cherry cokes, and spin on the red stools.

Pop paid at the cash register, "I'll take a Hav-a-Tampa cigar and a Mounds bar. We had two blue plate specials and ...don't forget the postcard. Thank you, Miss Ida Mae."

"You boys have a good day," She waved at they walked out the door.

Pop put his cigar in his top pocket, and Johnny did the same with his candy bar. Pop gave him a copper penny to buy a stamp from the postmaster, and then he dropped the postcard in the slot.

"You better eat your bar before it melts." Pop smiled as they drove a few blocks toward the railway tracks; where the seed and feed store was.

Johnny sat in the shade and ate his candy. The chocolate had melted onto the wrapper and all over his hands. He licked his fingers and wiped them on his jean shorts.

Allen's Seed and Feed was a gathering place for the men folk, especially farmers. While the men talked, he jumped on and off the loading dock.

"It's a hot one today!"

"Yes, sir. I think it's hot enough to fry an egg on the side walk."

They spoke in the same slow southern drawl Mr. Emil used. Then they took out their handkerchiefs and wiped the sweat from their brows. If someone had a nickel, they would put it in the cooler and take out a bottle of Coca-Cola to cool their throats.

"Pop, do ya' have a nickel?"

"What for?" As if he did not know.

"I'm thirsty," Johnny said.

"You just had a cherry Coke at the drug store."

"I know, but the Mounds bar made me extra thirsty. Besides it's hot enough to fry an egg on the side walk," Johnny gave Pop a convincing smile; who then reached into his pocket.

After the men agreed it was hotter than 'blazes' *and* the hottest summer on record, they moved on to their next favorite topic-- fishing. Who caught the biggest, where was it caught, and what kind of bait was it caught with? Was it a largemouth bass or a catfish? One told how a pointy-nosed gar had broken his line.

The men had more than enough places to fish. There were twenty-seven lakes on the Tsala Apopka chain connected to the Withlacoochee. They could fish in the lime-green waters of abandoned phosphate pits, clear springs, or even salt water if they went to the west side of the county. Johnny knew who caught the biggest fish and in what year.

Each man liked to say, "I heard the fishin' is good at--," and then fill in the blank.

If you went into town on a Wednesday afternoon all the shops and stores were closed. A hand written sign hung on the doors, which read, "Gone Fishin'." Well, they might have gone fishing, or they might have scoped out their neighbors' secret fishing spot--a little 'friendly' competition.

Johnny knew no man was going to share his 'secret' fishing hole. They might just say any old place so that no one would come to their spot. Mr. Emil, Pop and Johnny swore the location of their fishing hole to secrecy.

Pop would say, "Do you think we want half the county showing up?"

More than half the county did show up at the Fourth of July fish fry celebration. Musicians played banjos, harmonicas, and a trumpet, and someone even played a washtub. The music was lively, fast-paced blowing and strumming, so feet just had to dance. If a body was not dancing, it was lobbing a fishing line in the water. Arms flung out filament, and cane poles shimmied and shook along the shore. Boppers dipped under quickly, arms yanked, and pan fish went flying!

Pop, Mr. Emil, and Johnny put their fish on a stringer.

Mr. Dale, the tall and lanky photographer for the local paper, asked, "Would you look at that stringer? Can I take a picture for the paper?"

Johnny needed two hands to hold the string of fish.

"Say Fish!" *Click.* "Thank ya'll."

They carried their stringer over to the men, who had an assembly line for cleaning the fish. Then they passed it to the women, who coated them in cracker meal and fried them in huge skillets of hot fat. Johnny stood in the serving line for a plate full of the tender, crunchy, hot pan fish. It tasted sweet and delicious.

Under the shade trees, tables were set with slaws, salads, and pies. All types of pies baked fresh, including blackberry, mulberry, gooseberry, and blueberry. How could anybody decide? Johnny decided to try a slice of each.

"Son, every time I see you, you have a different kind of berry pie in your hand!" Pop laughed.

When he went to bed that night, he had a stomachache. If Mother were there, she would have given him a hot water bottle to soothe his too-much-berry-pie-tummy.

Johnny loved to fish, and he loved digging for worms almost as much. In the evenings, he dug around the roots underneath palmettos for worms. The dirt felt cool and slightly damp underneath the leaves. He tapped his fingers like rain in a ceremonial ritual, coaxing the worms closer to the surface. He rooted his shovel into the dirt like an armadillo's snout. Sometimes he heard armadillos digging for their dinner outside his window at night. Johnny filled his coffee can with worms and dirt, and then covered the top with damp moss. His can of worms was ready in the shade under the porch for the next day.

He and Pop fished in their backyard, standing barefoot in the shallow. Minnows came up and nibbled their toes if they stood in one place too long. Pop taught Johnny to cast a rod and reel, but he tangled it in the pickerel weed and lily pads or sent the line spinning around an oak branch hung over the water.

"I like my cane pole best," he said while he untangled his line again.

Pop cast his reel out into deeper water. Johnny sat on the fence built to keep the cows in and the gators out. He baited his hook with a worm and dangled it in front of a bluegill or catfish hoping they would bite. Pop cast once more near some lily pads and caught a largemouth bass for supper. They fished until they could no longer see to bait their hooks. When the mosquitoes were doing the biting, it was time to stop.

After chores the next morning, Johnny dug for his daily worms and saved the fattest worms under the porch. They were going fishing in their *secret* spot. Pop promised to take Johnny that afternoon, and he did not want anything to happen to his worms.

Johnny asked, "Pop, do you think an armadillo will knock over my can for a free meal? I heard them rooting around last night under my window."

"Not sure, but you can set them in the truck if you're worried," Pop laughed.

"Good idea." He put his can of worms on the front seat.

Whooo- Whooo.

A little owl turned his head, watching him, still awake from the night.

"Hey! No peeking!" He shook his finger at the owl. "And don't you tell."

When he ran into the house, the screen door slammed behind him. "I can't wait for later."

"Oh? What's happening later?" Pop pretended not to know.

"You and Mr. Emil are taking me to our secret fishing spot," he whispered.

"Well, we better get goin' then," Pop whispered back.

Later, Pop drove off the gravel road onto a narrow, sandy path between the palmettos. At the edge of the property, a weathered sign was nailed to a tree.

"Private property. Keep out," Johnny read out loud.

"That's grandfather's old sign," Pop said. "Looks like Mr. Emil beat us to it."

He followed fresh tire tracks made in the soft gray sand through the thicket, which scratched and pinged against the side of his truck. Oscee's tongue hung out of his mouth, panting the heat away. Johnny forgot about the heat and humidity until Oscee reminded him.

"Do you think it's goin' to rain this afternoon," he asked.

"Hope so. Our new trees need it, and the fish bite better," Pop winked.

He parked next to Mr. Emil's truck in an open sandy area. Johnny smelled Mr. Emil's cigar and saw two men standing at the lake edge. Johnny gasped, "Oh, my gosh! Grandfather! Pop! Grandfather's here!" He yelled and ran toward them. "What are you doin' here? Is Mother with you? Is Grandmother here? Are you fishin', too?"

He plowed into Grandfather with a big hug.

"Whoa, slow down," Grandfather said. "My goodness; look at you! Suntanned, barefoot, and a few inches taller. I hardly recognize you."

"Is Mother here?" He asked, out of breath.

"No," Grandfather said.

"Oh…" Johnny said, disappointed.

"I'm here on business. I had to check in with my Ocala office," Grandfather said. "Hello, John."

The men shook hands.

"Hello, Howard. I didn't know you were coming. How is the rest of the family?" Pop asked.

"They're fine, thank you for asking," Grandfather cleared his throat. "I heard about your plans to start a grove."

Johnny interrupted. "Yes sir, we have! But now we're goin' fishin'. I dug enough worms. Can you stay? Can you fish with us?" Then, in a whispered voice, "This is our secret spot. Were ya'll followed?"

"Ya'll? And since when did you start leaving off your 'g's? I wonder what Mother will say about that?" Grandfather said, half-teasing.

"Can we fish now, Pop?"

Mr. Emil said, "Johnny, come with me. I want to show you somethin'."

"But I thought we were goin' to fish," Johnny said, confused.

"We will. Let me show you something first."

The two of them walked off toward the bluff, leaving Grandfather and Pop to talk privately.

"I did come on business, but it was also a good excuse for me to check on my grandson."

Grandfather was a straightforward man. If something needed saying, he said it.

"I'm sorry to hear things aren't going well in your marriage," Grandfather said. "When we signed the papers, you didn't tell me you had plans to go into the citrus business. Citrus? You're a man with common sense. I've always trusted your judgment over the years." Grandfather lifted one eyebrow and said, "But citrus is a risky investment."

Pop listened to his father-in-law but did not speak. At that moment, there was no need to defend his decision.

Grandfather continued, "When I was a young man, the citrus industry boomed in this area. The groves shipped fruit through the canal, up the Withlacoochee to Lake Panosoffkee, and loaded trains for the east coast. A friend of mine thought about investing in the fruit market, but the freezes of 1883 and 1895 scared him off. Two winters of icicles on the trees froze their dreams. The growers and investors were left with nothing."

"They still had their land. You always told me that was the best investment a man could make," John said. "Our grove is small compared to others. It's not a sure thing, but what is? Not the stock market. By the way, we planted this summer. Maybe you could come over to see what Johnny and I have done with the place."

"Yes, I want to," Grandfather replied.

"I know it's a risk, Howard, and I might be frozen out someday."

"I have taken risks, too. Sometimes it has worked, and sometimes it hasn't," Grandfather said thoughtfully. "You are right; there are no guarantees--not in citrus, and not in phosphate. After World War One, the market demand in Europe fell, and our small mine hit water. We follow our instincts and hope for the best. I do wish you that, son."

"Thank you, sir. I'm grateful you helped give me the chance," John responded.

"I do hope the two of you can work something out. I only want my daughter's happiness." Grandfather's white cotton shirt was wet with perspiration. He took a monogrammed handkerchief out of his pocket and wiped his brow. "Why do you want to live here year round? I don't think I could ever get used to this heat."

"It can get hot up the country, too," Pop reminded him.

"True. It just doesn't last as long." Grandfather looked across the lake and asked, "Where did they go?"

"They probably walked over to the bluff. Do you see it?" Pop pointed.

Mr. Emil and Johnny reached the bluff underneath oak trees.

"Look here. Do you see this?" Mr. Emil pointed, "Rub your hand here where the bark is bulged out."

"What made this?" Johnny asked

"A cannon. This old tree was wounded in battle. The ol' timers around here call it the 'landmark tree'," Mr. Emil said.

"Another battle here?" Johnny asked. "On our land?"

He remembered the 1840 map Pop had shown him before they took their canoe excursion. The map of Florida during the Second Seminole War--the one with X's, which marked the battles in the cove. He had learned what happened at Fort Drane, Fort King, Dade's massacre, Clinch's and Gaines's battles along the Withlacoochee. If he drew a straight line from the river to the X marking Fort Cooper it would be about six miles through swamp and slough in between.

"Fort Cooper was here!" Mr. Emil exclaimed.

"Where?" Johnny felt the tree again then walked up and down the bluff. He walked to the bank, looking down at the ground. I can't tell anything happened here."

"Johnny, what are you looking for?" Mr. Emil asked.

"Another X... you know, an X that marks the spot. Like in Treasure Island, when Jim Hawkins found the pirate treasure." Johnny was half kidding and half serious.

What treasure was buried here, and was there really a fort? Did Osceola walk their farmland over a hundred years ago? Johnny wondered. "The landmark tree has to be a clue," he said confident.

"I believe it to be true," Mr. Emil said. "Ever since I was a young'un, I've heard stories about Osceola and his warriors and Major Cooper and his Georgia militia. I've heard they built a picket here. Some of the soldiers from General's Scott's campaign were left here after their battle on the Withlacoochee."

"The battles on the river...in the fog?" Johnny asked with wide eyes.

"Yes, Clinch, Gaines, and Scott fought a battle along the river. After Scott's battle, soldiers were left here. Let me show you something else--another clue."

They walked down the slope to the water. Johnny knelt down and cupped his hands over a small spring. White sand bubbled out of its way.

"Go ahead; taste it. It's good water--not like the sulphur water at the farm."

Johnny sipped it. "It's good and cool. How's this a clue?"

"They came because of the spring," Mr. Emil said.

"They? Who are they?"

"Indians, soldiers, and settlers... People just like us have been comin' out here for a long time. Folks have been tellin' tales about this bluff for almost a hundred years."

"I thought this was our secret fishin' spot?"

"It still is but it's a hand-me-down secret. My Granddaddy brought me here to fish and when it got too hot; we went skinny-dippin' to cool off," Mr. Emil laughed.

"There's something else different about this lake. It's not dark like ours," Johnny noticed. "How come?"

"Since it's spring fed, it's not a part of the chain of lakes. It stands all by itself. The Indians called it Lake Holathlikaha, meaning shining or grassy waters," Mr. Emil answered.

"I think it must mean both. It's shiny and grassy. Lake Ho-lath-lee-ka-ha," Johnny repeated the name.

"The Seminoles came to the cove after they had been pushed off their land in north Florida," Mr. Emil said.

"Where is the cove exactly? Pop talked about it when we were on the Withlacoochee."

"The river makes a curve, which is considered part of the cove, but the cove is an area, which includes lakes, islands, prairie, hammocks, swamps, and the slough."

"Here?" Johnny asked.

"For sure, here," Mr. Emil answered.

Johnny thought, what could have been... *Soldiers filled their metal cups or canteens with water from the spring. Seminoles brought their cattle to drink. Maybe women carried vessels taking fresh, clear water back to their village. Perhaps in a peaceful time, a young Seminole boy had come to fish in this secret spot with his father. Just like him.*

"Who were the militia?" Johnny asked.

Mr. Emil explained, "They were volunteers--civilian soldiers, not government soldiers--who took up arms for the cause. The Georgia militia was under the command of Major Mark Anthony Cooper."

"We better go back. The fish are waitin'," Johnny said. They walked back toward the trucks, and he looked back through the trees where they had come from. A white feather flashed quickly from behind a tree; he was sure of it. "Mr. Emil!" he called, and ran toward the big man in blue denim overalls. Johnny spent the afternoon with the three most important men in his life, Mr. Emil, Grandfather and Pop.

"How long has it been since you fished, Howard?" Pop asked.

"I'm ashamed to say too long," Grandfather answered. "It's so peaceful here; reminds me of what Florida was like when I was a boy. Seen any panthers out here, Johnny?"

"No, sir. No red wolf either, although I heard a black bear was seen down on the Bigelow place." Johnny cast out his line.

Something big jerked his pole. His bobber went under--really under! Then it disappeared in the lily pads. The line pulled so tight that he dug his heels into the sand. "Pop! What do I do?" he yelled holding, on with both hands. "I can't hold it!"

The men coached him how to pull the monster fish in.

"Calm down. Hold on. Don't let it get away!" They encouraged.

Pop stepped into the water and walked toward the line with a net.

"Walk backwards, son. Don't let go!"

"Grandfather, help me!" He hollered with excitement.

"Hold it steady!"

"Good boy. That's it." Pop slipped the net and reached into the water underneath the fish. "I see it son, it's a big one. You caught dinner tonight."

"I did. What is it?" Johnny asked with much excitement and out of breath.

"Largemouth bass," Pop answered. "He put up quite a fight."

Once the bass was secured in the net, it flipped his tail back and forth. Johnny threw down his pole and ran to help Pop carry it to the shore.

"Congratulations!" Grandfather said, "It sure is a big one!"

"Wait 'til the fellers hear about this. You definitely caught the biggest," Mr. Emil chuckled.

"Would you like to stay for dinner Howard?" Pop asked.

"I don't have any plans tonight. I'd love to," Grandfather said.

Lake Holathlikaha *was* the best fishing in the county, but Johnny would never tell.

Chapter 16

A week later, after their morning route, Pop said, "I've got a treat for breakfast this morning. Mr. Edwin gave us bacon as barter for milk and eggs." He set the slab of sugar-cured bacon on the seat, wrapped in brown paper and string. "Mr. Edwin has the best bacon you'll ever taste. We'll have to ration this out so we can get more meals out of it."

"What does 'ration' mean?" Johnny asked.

"A ration is the amount of food allotted per person per day. In these hard times, people have to think about rationing their supplies. Especially when they're not sure when their next meal comes from. It seems we waste more when times are good."

"How much do you think this weighs?"

"Maybe two pounds. It'll last a few weeks if we ration," Pop answered. "The military rationed food for soldiers, which is how a quartermaster figured out how much to supply the troops."

Pop began breakfast. He sliced two thick strips off the slab, and laid them in a hot iron skillet. The bacon sizzled as soon as it touched the pan. The fat popped and bubbled until it turned brown and crispy. The aroma made Johnny's taste buds crave his first bite.

"During nineteenth century wars, soldiers were rationed twenty ounces of beef. In the Second Seminole War, General Scott ordered bacon or salt pork instead of beef. Bacon weighed less, so it was the meat of choice," Pop explained.

"Twenty ounces," Johnny stated, "That's over a pound. It seems like a lot…"

"Well, don't forget the men marched many miles through treacherous terrain and fought Indians. Supplies were hard to come by. When an express rider or boat sent orders, it took weeks to get to the right person. Then, if the quartermaster received the order, he had to ship thousands of pounds of rations by steamboats on the rivers. Even then, supplies didn't always make it to the interior forts. Besides bacon, they also had flour or hardtack, which was like a thick cracker. Soldiers still have hardtack in their rations."

"What other things did soldiers have in their haversack?" Johnny asked.

"Vinegar, beans, salt, soap, candles, and most important, their coffee," Pop smiled.

"Pop, your coffee is sputterin'!" Johnny yelled.

Pop grabbed the handle of the blue enamelware coffee pot and pulled it off the flames. It spewed coffee grinds all over the place.

"What a mess! We'll let the grinds settle…."

"Can I do that, Pop? Can I eat rations like the soldiers did?" Johnny asked.

He packed a small canvas knapsack with saltine crackers, a pinch of salt wrapped in waxed paper, and a candle. He cut a piece of lye soap off a large bar then poured himself a cup of coffee. He wrapped his slice of bacon and grabbed a can of beans.

"Do we have any vinegar?" Johnny asked.

"Here," Pop said. "I'll pour some into a smaller bottle for you. There, you're all set. Are you going to eat outside?"

"Yes, sir." The screen door slammed behind him.

Johnny leaned against a tree in the front yard and opened his pack. He took a bite of the smoked, sugar-cured bacon. It was chewy and crunchy at the same time. He enjoyed every bite. Coffee was not his favorite drink, especially without a lump of sugar, but if he were going to be a real soldier; he would have to drink it black--grinds and all.

***

For Gaines's men, the bacon had run out a long time ago. They never got the provisions he requested. Gaines led his troop of gaunt-looking men into Fort Drane on March eighth. Most of them were brought in by wagons. They could barely walk, as they were sick or wounded. For those who could, they looked like walking skeletons. The soldiers at the fort pitied them, tossing them biscuits, which they devoured. The men were so hungry, they ate horse feed off the ground. Within a few days, General Gaines turned his troops over to Clinch, and had to wait in Fort Drane before following orders to his next assignment out west.

General Winfield Scott was on his way to Fort Drane. It had taken him over a month to travel from Washington to Picolata in the Florida territory. In the meantime, he sent orders to Washington requesting supplies. He wrote letters to southern governors asking for more men.

"Lieutenant," General Scott said, "tomorrow, we arrive in Picolata. I am quite certain we can drive the Seminoles from their stronghold. Governor Eaton has written me that there must be at least, if not more, three thousand Seminoles hidden in the cove. They have romped across the frontier and frightened poor settlers. My three-prong plan has to work. After all, what others have tried has failed. Now we just need the extra men to make it happen."

"Yes, sir, your letters have been sent expressing your request for more volunteers. Since the news of Dade's massacre has reached the rest of the country, I don't think you'll have a problem finding men to fight this war," the lieutenant responded.

"Good work, Lieutenant," General Scott said. He added with disdain, "Gaines is in *my* territory. I'm concerned that his presence will spoil any chance we have for surprise."

The steamer traveled on the St. Johns River and arrived in

Picolata in late February. The tall, heavily-built general stepped off the steamboat. He was dressed in his thick, wool military coat over his blue jacket, which was decorated with shiny brass buttons and a high collar. He wore ivory gloves and wool slacks tucked into shiny, high black boots. One shoulder fit squarely into the seam of his jacket decorated with gold tassels. The other shoulder was thrust slightly forward from an injury he had received in battle. When he stood in command of his men, he forced his shoulders back straight and stiff. His full, rounded chin granted him the look of royalty. His curved jowl was covered with waves of thick hair. When he became angry, he expounded on words too severe for the tender ears of delicate women and innocent children, but many a soldier heard them. His eyes could pierce an unruly man or soften a wounded soldier's heart.

Once he stood on the solid ground of his new department, the Florida wilderness was transformed. The sounds of the wild wood were exchanged with a full military brass band to cheer the soldiers and bring gallantry of service to their primitive camp. Simple campstools sat upon by other generals were replaced with fine mahogany ladder-back chairs. He carried a white tent for his quarters and furnished it with an oak chest, and cherry dining table with clawed feet. He also brought with him large cask of wine and dined on finer foods, which a sutler provided for him.

The first person he saw in Picolata was the quartermaster. He wanted to check on the arrival of his supplies.

"I'm sorry, sir. I don't have a favorable report about your supplies."

"I'm disappointed to learn rations I requested are less than I expected," General Scott complained. "I requested about fifteen thousand men from neighboring states. Where are my supplies, sir? Why haven't they arrived?" He raised his voice in anger. "This is such an embarrassment. I expected everything and everyone to be ready to march by now."

"A few men have arrived, sir. Two companies from South

Carolina and one from Alabama. Major Cooper and his Georgia battalion arrived two weeks prior to your arrival," the quartermaster said nervously. "They're very anxious to start their march, too."

"A week ago, I requested from the quartermaster in Washington: fifty thousand rations of hard bread and ninety thousand rations of bacon for all the men in our campaign. Surely something has arrived by now," General Scott yelled.

"I'm sorry, sir. Some things have, but no bacon has arrived," the quartermaster told him. "I'm sure the supplies will be here soon."

"I hope you're right." The general said, optimistic but with sarcasm. "After all, President Jackson wants the Indians relocated or killed as soon as possible. He knows I can't run this war without men and rations."

As he left the quartermaster, he yelled, "I need *my* bacon!"

A few days later, General Scott met with Major Cooper of the Georgia militia. The Georgia volunteers had arrived in Picolata on February seventeenth.

"Major, I understand you have had your men ready and they are eager to march into the interior," General Scott greeted Major Cooper.

"Yes, sir, my men are ready," Major Cooper replied.

"Good, I like that in my troops," General Scott praised. "Major, tomorrow your battalion will march to Fort Drane. General Clinch is under constant skirmishing attacks by the Indians. Your orders are to act as reinforcement and wait for me. When I'm certain that the necessary rations have arrived, I'll join the right wing, and then we'll march to the Withlacoochee River."

"Yes, General, my men will be glad to hear the good news. They're tired of sitting with nothing to do. They're fine young men, sir, and a good lot of southern gentlemen," Major Cooper said proudly.

The next day, the Georgia militia began their march along the military road. Their uniforms were simple--tow shirts and overalls with their knapsacks strapped to their backs. They had only marched a day when an express rider charged down the road after them.

"Major Cooper?" the rider asked.

"Yes, I'm he," the major answered.

"New orders from General Scott." He reached in his leather pouch and handed the major a sealed letter.

"Much obliged, sir."

Major Cooper read the message out loud to his men. *"You must return to Picolata at once. I fear that I have misjudged the amount of provisions at Fort Drane. I'm recalling your men to prevent starvation. General Clinch barely has enough rations for his men. Signed, General Winfield Scott."*

There were moans from the militia. Frustrated and disappointed, the men shouted.

"I bet they smelled a rat all the way in Putnam," a Georgian exclaimed.

"Hear, hear!" Voices cheered.

"That's all; a march in to the woods and back to camp?"

"What for? Because there aren't enough rations?"

"We're prepared to eat only when hungry, sir."

"We'll march hungry…in heat, on bad roads. As long as we're marching."

"Please, give us something to do."

"For how much longer?"

"We can't just go back and sit."

"It's already been two weeks."

"I'm ready to fight the Indians."

"Give us a chance."

"Men," Major Cooper said calmly, "I'm just as disappointed as you, but we need to follow these orders. Our time will come, gentlemen; you'll see. I'm proud to march with you, and I thank you for electing me as your commander. We'll turn around and march from whence we came."

Meanwhile, after Clinch's defeat, he sat in Fort Drane waiting for General Scott to arrive. He read a message Osceola had sent him. He read it over and over again.

You have guns, and so have we. You have powder, and lead and so have we. You have men, and so have we. Your men will fight, and so will ours, until the last drop of Seminoles' blood has moistened the dust of his hunting grounds.

Each time he read those powerful words from the Seminole chief, he knew he had underestimated Osceola's passion as a patriot.

I have miscalculated his abilities as a soldier and his love for his homeland. Even so, I expect General Scott and the rest of the troops soon. However, I am cautious. Does the general know what he is up against? Clinch thought.

The heavy rains in early March made everything worse. In Fort Drane, General Clinch waited for General Scott. Major Cooper and the Georgia militia waited for their chance. General Scott continued to wait for his bacon. It rained, and it rained, and it rained.

"The rivers are swollen. Such an obstacle makes transportation impossible. I've wagons coming from Baltimore. I heard Gaines took some of my rations. My horses haven't left Savannah for the baggage train. And to affront my campaign further...there's no bacon!" General Scott yelled and complained.

A few days later, it was still raining. The general stomped in deep puddles and stood in front of the quartermaster. He was dripping wet. "Where's my bacon?" he demanded and slammed his fist on the table, which bounced damp papers and an ink well.

"I'm sorry, sir. I haven't heard anything. The weather has caused dilatory," the quartermaster said nervously. "I can dispatch another request, sir."

The conditions in Picolata were miserable. Soldiers and militia were soaked from the rain. Some men had tents; others crowded in the few buildings or small booths made out of palmetto fronds to keep the water off their backs.

"It's bad enough we're soaked to the skin every night, but worse, we have nothing to do," the men complained to Major Cooper.

The wood was too wet, and it was hard to keep the fires going.

The flour became damp and infested with mealy bugs. Hard tack and cold beans had to sustain them.

"I'll talk to the general," he promised.

That evening, Major Cooper went to the general's tent. "Permission to come in, sir."

"Yes, by all means. What can I do for you?" the general responded.

"My men are good soldiers," said Major Cooper.

"I'm sure they're fine men."

"They feel they'll miss out on your campaign. They're eager to march with you," Major Cooper stated emphatically.

"Bring your men to me in formation tomorrow morning," General Scott ordered.

The next morning, the First Georgia Battalion stood in formation in the mud. The General, dressed in his full military uniform, paraded before them and inspected the troops.

"Men you look to me to be fine soldiers. We'll be marching very soon. I'd like very much for you to go with me and have the post of honor," General Scott promised. "I appreciate your waiting."

The men cheered loudly. It was just what they needed to hear. Finally, they would be able to serve their country. His speech gave them the hope they needed. They could focus on the march instead of how wet and hungry they were.

At last, the supplies from Savannah arrived. The quartermaster reported to Scott, "We only received twelve thousand seven hundred forty rations of hard bread and twenty-one thousand six hundred rations of bacon, seventeen thousand nine hundred forty-seven rations of flour and eleven thousand rations of pork."

"It's not exactly what I requested. We agreed hard bread and bacon is a better choice for the march," Scott criticized. "Instead, they sent me more flour and pork. How does Washington expect me to carry out my campaign in this terrain if I do not have the correct rations? As it is, we only have about six days' worth."

"We had no choice but to make up the difference with flour and pork, sir," the quartermaster replied.

"As if Gaines' intrusion into my command isn't bad enough," he grumbled. "I hope the sutlers can make up the difference for us. In the meantime, when is this damn rain going to stop? How can I move my wagon trains to Fort Drane in this mud?" He stomped out angrily and shook his fist at the sky.

"Perhaps, sir, we can leave some men behind and wait for more supplies," the quartermaster suggested.

"Issue what rations we have--coffee, beans, and vinegar. Bacon or no bacon, rain or no rain; dispatch the men to march. Load the wagons and flat boats," General Scott ordered.

He left the tent and his black boots splashed through a big puddle. He grumbled to himself. "Insufficient rations of hard bread and bacon. How can I win a war with no bacon? Leave some men behind. Wait for more supplies. General Clinch is waiting. I'll not wait another day."

Two days after General Scott promised the Georgia volunteers a post of honor in his march to Fort Drane, he left without them. The news caught Major Cooper off guard and deflated his tall, commanding appearance.

I kissed my wife and children goodbye for this? He thought to himself. *I willingly left them to serve my country, not to sit idle and do nothing.*

"General Gaines was surrounded by the enemy and at the point of starvation," Major Cooper told his men, "but we have been left ignobly on the banks of the St. Johns River for six weeks." He added with sympathy, "We've been left under the dominion of General Eustis, commander of the left wing."

The men from Georgia looked at each other in disbelief. They could not have heard the major correctly. Surely, he did not just tell them they had been left behind. After the shock moved through the militia, a volunteer from Bibb County yelled, "But we were assigned to march with the right wing!"

"What're we going to do, sir?" Captain Foster asked.

"Sir, I'm tired of camp life. Maybe we shouldn't have come. If I was home now, I'd be plowin' my red fields and plantin'. Instead I'm sittin' here doin' nothin' and waitin' to kill red men I'll never see," a young farmer complained.

"Do we head back to Georgia?" Another asked.

"Men, I've a few things to take care of. Prepare yourselves to march," Major Cooper reassured them. "Captain, find me a small boat."

General Scott ordered General Eustis to command Scott's left wing and stay in Picolata until more rations arrived. Major Cooper took two of his men in the boat, and they crossed the river to talk to General Eustis.

General Eustis saw the men approaching. *What now,* he thought.

"General Scott's three-pronged campaign has begun, Major," General Eustis said.

"Yes, sir, I'm aware of that," Major Cooper replied. "And we're both still here."

"I've been ordered not to send troops forward until we have sufficient rations for three days beyond Fort Drane. There are no rations or transportation that can be provided for the Georgia battalion," General Eustis stated firmly.

"General Eustis, we'll march forward tomorrow," Major Cooper said emphatically.

"Surely not without orders."

"With or without orders, General, we *will* march," Major Cooper replied with confidence.

Major Cooper and his men got into the boat to cross back over the river. He spotted some horses on the bank. "Tell the captains to form companies and encircle the horses."

"Yes, sir," the citizen soldier replied.

"Tell them to detail two men from each company to harness the horses and take the best wagons to camp." The tall Major's long legs swung out of the boat. He stepped foot on the muddy bank and smiled. "Gentlemen, I have a plan."

The rest of the day was spent getting ready to march towards Fort Drane. They rebuilt the wagons, harnessed the horses, and loaded up wagons with gear.

"In January, I requested supplies and bacon from Governor Schley. He knows how to take care of his Georgia boys. He has sent us three thousand pounds of our own Georgia bacon. It's been on reserve for us until it could be salt cured and dried."

"How come General Scott did not find it in camp?" A curious soldier asked.

Major Cooper smiled. "It wasn't sent to him. The quartermaster wouldn't have known about it because it's not government property. Besides, the government isn't going to provide for us. We had to bring our own guns and ammunition, didn't we? So we can bring our own bacon."

The men cheered. They could not go another day being idle and feeling helpless. The next few days they had something to do, following orders; their tasks brought them from despair and doubt to joy and certainty. They had left their farms and families for the jungle of Florida for a purpose. Major Cooper and his five companies--"A" Company, State Fencibles; "B" Company, Macon Volunteers; "C" Company, Monroe Musketeers; "D" Company, Hancock Blues; and the "E" Company, Morgan Guard--marched on the military road to Fort Drane with such determination they covered seventy miles in twenty-six hours. They would not miss their opportunity to enter the campaign this time.

The major saw a party on horseback waiting up ahead for them. He was prepared for anything, but he and his men would not be sent back. General Scott, General Clinch and their staff, sat tall in their saddles. "Here come the Georgia Boys. Welcome to Fort Drane."

"General Scott, General Clinch," Major Cooper addressed them politely.

General Scott was impressed with their determination to follow him. "Yes, Major, I do believe you have the finest four hundred men in the country." General Scott saluted them and led them toward

Fort Drane with a hesitant smile. "You made sure I kept my word. We leave in the morning."

Later in the day, the soldiers fried their dough and salt pork over their campfires and boiled their green coffee. On the other side of the pines, the Georgia militia set up their bivouac and cooked their Georgia bacon over their fires. Their smoky campfire burned and crackled from the damp wood. The men cooked their bacon on sticks held over the fire, and the aroma from the sizzling bacon blended with the damp piney wood, which wafted over Fort Drane. The smell of dripping fat gnawed at their stomachs. The men had worked up an appetite from their long, hard march from Picolata, and they were hungry. When they ate the smoked, sugar-cured, salted bacon, it was chewy and crunchy at the same time; they enjoyed every bite. They drank their coffee black, grinds and all.

Chapter 17

Meanwhile, General Scott and his staff dined on vegetable soup, potato biscuits, and wild turkey in the officer's tent.

"Gentlemen," General Scott raised his wine glass, "a toast to this fine meal provided by the sutler." "Here, here," the officers chimed in. He raised his glass again, "and to my three-prong plan, which is already in operation." The officers clinked their glasses again. General Scott explained, "The left wing, commanded by General Abraham Eustis, has four artillery companies and is waiting for supplies, one company of South Carolina volunteers, and one regular infantry company. The center wing, commanded by Colonel William Lindsey, has left Fort Brooke and is marching north toward the cove. General Clinch and I'll be commanding the right wing, which Major Cooper and his battalion have joined. They add an additional three hundred eighty men to our troops. My strategy is designed to advance on the Seminoles while they flee from us, the other two wings will be able to encircle and cut them off, and thus the war will be won."

The officers around the cherry dining table clapped for General Scott.

"To victory!" the officers chanted and clinked their glasses again.

General Clinch said, "Since I experienced difficulty crossing the ford in December, I supervised the building of two flat boats, General. They've been loaded on wagon frames and already taken to the river ahead of us."

"Thank you, General. I'm sure the river is more swollen since the rain. Shall we have the band play tonight?" Scott asked, "I think it'll encourage the troops."

The staff nodded in agreement.

"But before we do, I want to make one more toast to Gaines, who is on his way out west." General Scott drank his toast with great satisfaction. "Most uncomfortable having him in my territory."

"Excuse me, sir," a second lieutenant interrupted.

"Yes, this better be important," General Scott grumbled.

The young lieutenant whispered something in the general's ear-- such news that the General Scott slammed his fist on the table. The dishes and utensils clattered and clicked from the vibration.

"Well, I'll be damned! Major Cooper has *my* bacon. Bring him here at once," he yelled. "Send my aide to tell him to turn over my bacon."

The aide went to the encampment of the Georgians. "Major, orders from General Scott: give him his bacon at once."

The major stood and calmly looked the young man in the eye. "I, sir, will decline to obey that order."

The aide walked back to the general's tent, trembling with fearfulness. Flustered, he stumbled and stammered. The general heard his gibberish words.

"Speak up! What did the major say?"

"He declines, sir," and then braced for the outraged response.

"I will not tolerate such disobedience," General Scott shouted. "You tell him at once to turn over my bacon."

Again, Major Cooper refused to hand over the Georgia bacon. His response ensued another order from the general. He was to report to the general at nine o'clock in the morning.

The next morning, Major Cooper strapped on his sword. He

asked two of his trusted men to accompany him, saying, "I'm ordered to headquarters for refusing to give up the Georgia bacon. I don't know what will happen to me--maybe a summons for a court martial, but we will hold onto our bacon, come what may. You'll gird your swords and follow me. Say nothing and do nothing, but listen and attend to me. Do as I order and strike when and where I strike."

"We're ready, Major. We'll follow you."

Major Cooper looked each man in the eye then continued to headquarters with the control and poise. They stepped in to the large tent. General Scott and the rest of his staff were seated. General Clinch and his staff were also seated. They were all dressed in their full military uniforms, looking at Major Cooper with eyes of judgment.

"Major Cooper," said General Scott.

"I am here."

"Take a seat," said the general, and the major did.

"Major Cooper," Scott began, "You have a lot of bacon in your wagons, I'm informed. Is it so?"

"It is so, General."

"Major Cooper, I ordered you to turn that bacon over to the commissary of the army, and it was reported to me that you declined to obey the order. Is that so?"

"It's true, general, that I declined to obey that order."

"You have been mustered into U.S. service."

"I have."

"Have you read the Articles of War?"

"I have."

"Do you know the consequence of disobedience of orders in service?" Scott asked.

"I suppose I do," Cooper replied.

"What, then, have you to say in this case, Major Cooper?"

"I have this to say," Cooper answered. "I have not, in this instance, subjected myself to a penalty for violating the Articles of

War, since they embrace only cases, in which the order given is by an officer and relates to matter subject to his order. The order here violated relates to the Georgia bacon held by me for my men, which is not subject to the order of General Scott, for it isn't U.S. stores, isn't individual property on the way, but is private stores of the men and furnished by Governor Schley of Georgia for their use. Hence, I am bound to hold this bacon for their use against the order of General Scott."

General Giles spoke, "You've heard the case, gentlemen. What do you think?"

"This seems to be a rather serious case," General Clinch said. "Perhaps we can compromise. Major, since we are short of wagons, can you agree that your men should also march with an equal amount of supplies as the rest of the command?"

"Yes, sir, my men can march with equal supplies and wagons equal to rest of the command," Major Cooper agreed, but he was cautious. He knew the generals were after his bacon.

General Clinch continued, "It's hard to deprive the major of all the bacon sent to his men by the governor of Georgia. Perhaps this negotiation of equal supplies and wagons will settle our predicament."

Major Cooper nodded in agreement, but his strategy to save the bacon and share the wagons was already established in his mind.

"Good, then it's settled. Are you satisfied, General?" General Clinch addressed General Scott.

"Satisfactory," Scott answered quickly.

"Come, Major. Join us for a glass of wine."

"Excuse me, General. I do not drink wine," Major Cooper declined.

"Get your men ready. We'll march at seven in the morning," General Scott commanded.

The three men left the tent and walked over to their battalion. Purman and Brooking asked, "Sir, what is your plan? We got the feeling that they think you are going to share your wagons and the bacon. Are you?"

"Oh, I'll share the wagons; they just won't have any bacon loaded on them." Major Cooper smiled and called his captains together.

"Men we are in the campaign, and the bacon has been saved. The general's last words to me were, 'get your men ready,' so that is what we'll do. Have your men unload all the wagons. Choose the three best wagons and divide the bacon into thirds. Reload the three wagons with the bacon and any others necessities, and then burn the rest. Turn over the two empty wagons to the quartermaster. I do recall they said they were short and in need of extra." Major Cooper communicated his plan in his slow, southern speech with a twinkle in his eye, which reassured the captains.

The men followed his instructions, packed up, and stood in columns the next morning, ready to march.

The commissary came up to Major Cooper. "Sir, hand over our share of the bacon."

Major Cooper, composed, replied, "Our three wagons are loaded, and there was no bacon to turn over. The two empty wagons have already been turned over to the quartermaster."

The commissary just looked at him with a confused stare.

"Have you loaded my pipe of wine?" General Scott asked his commissary. "Bacon--do I have my wagons of bacon?"

"You have your wagons, sir, but there was no bacon left to turn over."

"Vexation!" General Scott looked down the column of men. Major Cooper, in command of the First Georgia Volunteer Battalion, was lined up to march.

He's got guts! I admire that in a soldier, General Scott thought. He had a war to win, with or without his bacon. This time it would be without bacon. There was nothing more to be said. He nudged his horse with his boots, and gave the order to the right wing.

"Forward, march!"

"The roads are mired thick, sir!" A soldier reported to General

Scott.

Heavy rains had already caused problems in Picolata, and the roads were impassable, especially for heavy wagons.

They had not traveled far when thick wheels sank into the mud. Captains yelled to their men, "Push! Pull!"

The march halted, and men grunted in their effort to push and pull the spokes out of the quagmire ground. Then someone shouted, "Loosen some boards off the wagons, and make a plank road."

This helped the lumbering wagons to move a little easier. Men picked up the boards from behind and placed them under the wheels. After the wagons passed, the men moved the boards ahead for the next length of road. The horses had towed so hard, their coats lathered.

"The horses are breaking down!" a soldier yelled.

"Rest the horses, but not too long. We got to keep moving!" a captain shouted.

Chapter 18

General Scott arrived at Fort Drane on March thirteenth. Unfortunately, he and General Gaines were stuck in the boundaries of the fort for one day.

"What's he doing here?" General Scott complained to General Clinch. "As if things weren't bad enough."

Even for a day, their presence together in the confines of Fort Drane was most uncomfortable. The troops noticed it, and the derision between the men passed through the ranks. Gaines left for the western territory in his worn, stained field clothes. He took victory with him, which in his mind had been achieved in the cove.

General Scott adopted a European battle plan, hoping to concentrate three divisions to surround the Seminoles and drive them out of the cove. His division included General Clinch's troops, along with the battalion of Georgia volunteers under Major Cooper and volunteers from other southern states and the regulars.

On March twenty-fifth, the day of departure, another heavy rain fell. They left a day later. General Scott ordered over two thousand men, "Forward, march!" toward Camp Izard. They had wagons loaded with fifteen days' worth of rations, packhorses, ample powder and shot, and two six-pound cannons. Each man wore his haversack, filled with three more days' worth of food. They carried a cartridge bag, and a rifle or musket. Each company had three tents to share.

Late on the twenty-eighth, General Clinch and General Scott's horses stood at attention next to each other.

"I'm not use to this country, General. What do you suggest?" Scott asked.

"Camp Izard is about two hundred yards away," Clinch pointed. "We should encamp here for the night."

"I hope we're early enough the Indians won't know we're here," said General Scott.

General Clinch knew the Seminoles better than any officer. "Trust me, sir, they know we're here."

He then ordered, "Colonel Gadsden, post sharp shooters and two cannons on the bank to protect our crossing. I've prepared, under my own direction, two flat boats, which were loaded on wagons and await us there."

"Yes, sir," Colonel Gadsden saluted. He rode off to find the best men for the job. Everything was in place by four a.m.

**

After the Fourth of July and Grandfather's visit, the summer began to wind down. The end of summer did not show signs of change indicating another season. The temperature certainly did not give a clue autumn would soon approach. Johnny knew he only had two weeks left before he had to take a night train back up north. Soon, he would be back in school, wearing scratchy wool knickers and starched shirts. His feet would be cramped into his shoes and walking through autumn leaves. He could not think of that, now. He was still in Florida, and wanted to go back to the landmark tree.

Mr. Emil's words played over in his mind. *Some of the soldiers from General's Scott's campaign were left there after their battle on the Withlacoochee. After Scott's battle, soldiers were left here, on their farm.* He knew it must be true. Osceola walked on their farm!

"Pop, can we go back to the river one more time before I leave?" Johnny asked.

"I don't want to think about you leaving, son," Pop said. "Did you want to go back after what happened last time?"

John was not ready for summer to end, either. He dreaded the drive back to Tampa's Union Station when he would have to say goodbye to his son. "Let's not talk about that right now," Pop said sadly.

"The river?" Johnny asked. "Or me leaving?"

"You leaving," Pop answered. "I'm sorry; yes, we can go back to the river."

"What was the take out place called?" Johnny asked.

"Blodget's Ferry," Pop answered.

"That's where I want to go back," Johnny said. "We don't have to stay all day. I just want to canoe a few hours. Can you talk to Mr. Emil? Do you think he would like to come with us?"

"I'll ask him," Pop replied. "That's a nice idea."

This time Mr. Emil went with Pop and Johnny, but they left Oscee behind. The skies were gray, and the air was muggy. Little lime-green tree frogs sang their rain song. Whenever they sang, rain was sure to follow.

"We may just get a little rain. I don't think it'll be too threatening," Pop said. "We'll keep our eyes and ears out for lightning and thunder. If it does, we'll come in. Water is a bad place to be in a lightning storm."

Mr. Emil sat in the stern, Pop sat in the bow, and Johnny sat in the middle. They paddled amongst the floating beds of water hyacinth. The amphibious meteorologists were right. It began to rain. Johnny watched the paddles dip in the water. Small water circles formed after each stroke. Water circles inside water circles, with drops of rain falling inside them. Mysterious concentric circles multiplied across the surface of the river. When the cool raindrops hit the warm water of the Withlacoochee, a fog arose in the swamp and enveloped them. They lifted the paddles out of the water, sat silently, and waited.

***

By four in the morning, everything was in place and quiet. Generals Scott and Clinch wanted to get the men shuttled across the river.

"We need a strong swimmer to attach a rope to the other side," General Gadsden said.

"I'll do it, sir," said Mr. Blodget. "It's a good thing it's dark. I figure the gators won't see me." He chuckled, took off his clothes and boots, leaving them on the bank.

"Can I have these?" one of his comrades teased.

"Don't worry; I'll be back," Mr. Blodget said. He tied his company flag around his head and stepped into the water while the guideline was anchored to a tree. Holding the other end between his teeth, he swam to the south bank of the river with his head out of the water. He stayed focused on the dark silhouette of saw grass and tree line. His arms and legs fanned out with forward and sideways strokes, making his body glide quietly in the water. He thought, *Swim silent. I don't want Indians takin' a shot at me.*

"Where is he? I don't see or hear him," a voice whispered from the bank.

"Do ya'll think a gator got him?" another hushed voice said. Those close by shoved the man who asked such an unpleasant question.

"We'd would've heard something," someone suggested.

Mr. Blodget felt the current pulling him away as he bit down harder on the rope. He breathed heavily with each stroke, pushing harder against the water to move forward. He felt weeds against his legs and groped for dry land. He pulled his body up on the bank to tie their flag and the rope securely to a tree. Once the men felt the rope taut across the river, they knew he had made it.

"General Scott," Captain Robertson reported, "Mr. Blodget made it across safely."

"Tell him to report to me," General Scott commanded.

The flat boats were loaded with regulars and Louisiana volunteers, and then another load of men, supplies, and weapons were ferried over. The men brought Mr. Blodget's dry clothes. He put on his overalls and boots and reported to General Scott.

"Mr. Blodget, satisfactory. Satisfactory performance. For your gallant effort and contribution to my campaign, I'm naming this crossing after you: Blodget's Ferry."

"Thank you, sir," Mr. Blodget humbly said. "I needed a bath anyway."

It took all day on March thirty-first to get the men over. One company found a ford further down the river, rode their horses across and met up with General Scott's campaign on the south bank. Men continued to cross the Withlacoochee River in the flat boats.

Clinch was right; the Seminoles knew they were there. Hidden, they watched, waited, and let them cross over. As the rear made the last crossing, the Seminoles seized the moment and fired from the other side. Warriors were situated on a little island in the middle of the river. They had a good advantage to fire upon the troops. The sharpshooters of the rear guard exchanged fire, and the cannons were discharged. The Withlacoochee River once again was riddled with rapid gunfire and cannonballs whizzing through the air.

"The Indians have quieted down. I'm a bit suspicious, General," said General Clinch.

"I'm beginning to suspect an erroneous calculation as to how many Indians are actually out here," replied General Scott.

"Oh, they're out there, General; you can be sure of that," Clinch assured him.

"My question is... How many?" Scott replied. "I'm convinced; the whole force of the enemy is not in this area. Even though we've been led to believe otherwise."

Toward evening, they crossed over to the north bank without any more gunfire and hid until the rear division made their final pass. Captain Black and the Monroe Musketeers crossed the river with one piece of artillery. At dusk, the shooting began from the north bank. Once again, gun smoke rose above the water. Without hesitation, the rear guard returned with gunfire and safely crossed. Then the Indians vanished into the palmettos, just like ghosts.

"Sir, should we return fire?" An officer asked.

"No, I don't think there are very many of them. Let it pass for now," General Scott replied.

What Scott did not realize was that Osceola and the other chiefs had their own plan. There were many attributes of the Seminoles, which their white enemy did not understand. One quality was their ability to adapt. If the white men were going to travel in three columns, they could reinvent their strategies and do the same. In council, they painted their faces in black and red, with green bands under their eyes to help them see in the dark. For those who wore only loin clothes into battle they painted streaks of red and black on their chest. They strapped on their knives and hatchets and carried their guns. They divided themselves, attacking the wings of troops around the edges of Scott's three-prong campaign.

During the night, the wind carried the sound of distant gunfire from the other wings. They were all about thirty miles from each other, but no word passed between the columns. The random sounds of an occasional gunfire kept the soldiers awake and on guard most of the night.

General Scott spoke privately with General Clinch. "My dear friend, great soldier, and Mr. President, once gave me this advice: 'Sir, I never detach against Indians.' Until now, I've taken his advice and based my three-prong plan on it. Since I've never been in the interior of Florida before, I've had to rely on reports from the governor and other officers. I was under the impression there has been a severe concentration of the enemy in the cove. I personally chose to command the right wing so I could see for myself what is forthcoming here. So far, I don't believe the number of Seminoles in the cove is accurate. They think they own this land, but they never paid for one acre of it. I'm not sure if it's worth time or effort to parley."

"Sir, often warriors ask to parley, but we can't trust them. It's been my experience they don't show up. If they do parley, they aren't the chiefs and have no say in decisions," General Clinch responded. "Look at what happened with General Gaines. In error, I came upon a parley with Osceola, who, I'm sure, was being ever so cunning. He perhaps wanted more time, asking for further council with other chiefs. He may have been tired of fighting, but he had no intentions of giving up his homeland."

General Scott added, "I've decided to disregard Mr. President's advice. I feel I can become bolder now and detach more freely."

"We certainly can cover more ground," General Clinch agreed.

"Notwithstanding, sir, all my frights and bugbears have left me," General Scott confessed. "Tomorrow, I'll divide the men to go beyond our support distance to search for, and do battle with, the enemy."

The next day, the columns moved through the cove until they reached a prairie near the chain of lakes.

"This must be the prairie we've heard reports about sir," General Scott said. "Halt the baggage train and guard it while the rest of the troops form a line for an attack."

For the next two days, he sent out several detachments to scour the area around the chain of lakes, which connected to the river. The soldiers searched through hammock, swamp, marshes, connecting ponds, islands, and prairie for the Seminoles. One infantry detachment ran into some Seminole fire exerting their movement through thick boggy muck while the natives ran over the marsh with ease. Another detachment saw a group of Seminoles on an island and pursued them for another four miles, but they too disappeared into the hammock. There were a few skirmishes and some questionable encounters, but the soldiers were growing frustrated with the nimble natives they had hoped to fight.

General Clinch ordered another detachment, "Men, form a line and move out."

The soldiers saw a small group of warriors on the other side of the prairie.

"This could be it," a soldier steadied himself.

"What do you mean? There aren't that many," another man questioned.

"The rest could be hidin' like they always do," said a veteran soldier.

"Get ready men. This could be a tight scratch," another man warned.

"Is this a surrender, or is this a gull?" a soldier asked, as he watched the party cross the prairie.

"The Indians move like they mean to fight," another man observed.

A Louisiana volunteer, an interpreter, and a friendly Indian guide went to meet them carrying a white flag. The Seminoles vanished when they saw the men coming toward them.

"Let's step back into the column. We can't take any chances," an officer commanded. "Charge!"

The troops charged into the prairie, but instead of finding warriors, they found a breakfast fire with a few uncooked doves.

"I guess we interrupted them," the interpreter said. "There couldn't be too many of them by the size of this meal."

"We better report this to General Scott," an officer counseled.

"These doves are another proof of risibility to this situation. I've satisfied my mind there are just a few forces in the area, perhaps 500 men--certainly not thousands," scoffed General Scott.

"We didn't get a good look at them, sir. It might have been some women-folk preparing a meal for their young 'uns," the volunteer said.

"The other detachments have reported some cold cook fires, abandoned towns, and signs of the Indians' cattle, but we cannot find any new trails, sir," another captain reported.

The second morning before sunrise, Colonel Bankhead spoke with Major Cooper. "Major, you're officer of the day. Your battalion is the advance guard. Seek out any Indians hidden in the prairie."

"Yes, sir."

"Line up men," Major ordered.

The men faced the sun in the quiet morning and walked on firm, dry ground. Tall grass scratched against their pant legs.

"I relish not walkin' in mud," one volunteer said.

"What's this?" One man tripped. "It felt like a cannonball."

A few men laughed. "Here's your cannonball."

The men looked down at the round, grayish-black shell of the gopher tortoise.

"Ya'll ain't gonna scare many Injuns wit' that. Keep movin'."

After the men passed the gopher, it pushed out its large head, flat front feet, and stubby back legs, pulling his heavy armor through prairie grass in the opposite direction.

The Georgia battalion marched in perfect unison with each other. A long line of men carrying guns looked like folded paper dolls strung out across the prairie.

"I don't see anyone, sir."

"I don't think they want us to see them," said Major Cooper. He cupped his hand over his brow, shading his eyes to get a better look at the prairie. "About eighty yards away, I see an abrupt wall of shrub."

Suddenly, the entire battalion fell into mud and water three feet deep. The slough slurped up each soldier and his gun as mud oozed into his boots. The enemy had been waiting and watching for the perfect opportunity. They had the advantage once again. The Seminoles had a plan behind their palmetto fortress.

"When the pale face falls, shoot your guns," a chief commanded his warriors. "The slough is our friend."

Major Cooper knew they were hidden behind the wall of palmetto shrub. Gunfire rang across the prairie and smoke rose above the fronds. He resolved a firm and deliberate order, and yelled "Charge!"

The command bounced down the line of men. Brave volunteers responded with such tenacity the slough released its grip and they sloshed mud forward toward the shrub. Once again, the Seminoles vanished, so Major Cooper returned to the main body. Other detachments also returned, reporting their events to General Scott.

"General, I have lost four men and have nine wounded. The men are getting frustrated. Every time they sally with the Indians, they disappear," General Clinch said.

"In the morning, we will march to Fort Brooke," General Scott replied. "It's pointless to pursue the Seminoles. We'll camp on the prairie tonight."

MURIEL TUTTLE EDEN-PAUL

Chapter 19

Johnny knew where Major Cooper and his Georgia militia would go after they left the river, slough, and prairie. Following the military map, they would travel by the bluff on Lake Holathlikaha. He wanted to go back there one more time.

***

The morning of April first, 1836, the right wing marched through the woods on the military road. Some soldiers were glad to head towards Fort Brooke. The volunteers thought of going home. Some were disappointed they had not seen more fighting. The columns marched on firmer ground of sandy soil through scrub palmetto and yellow pine. Overhead, the sunlight shone brighter in the pinewoods than in the hammock. The heat of the morning sun warmed the men. Their shirts were stained with sweat and mud, and some were bloody from shallow wounds. Blue jays screeched at the sound of wagon wheels, hoofs, and heavy steps of tired men. Squirrels scampered overhead from one tree to another scolding the troops. Even though their enemy could attack them anytime, the woods seemed less daunting than the swamp. The column had traveled about ten miles and came upon a small crystal clear lake.

General Scott shouted, "Halt! At ease, men. Water the horses and oxen; fill the barrels with fresh water. The water quality looks better here than we've seen in a while."

As he had already discussed with General Clinch, he changed his plans. He was going to leave a detachment and take his troops to Fort Brooke. They had begun to fatigue from their swamp marches, poor water, and sleepless nights. They were deprived of proper nutrition because of minimal rations of flour and pork. They had no hard bread, and no bacon, which General Scott recanted over and over; was not his fault but the inadequacy of others. He rode his horse down the columns of men and stopped in front of Major Cooper.

"Major Cooper," he said, "I've been impressed with your leadership and the quality of your men. They're not just volunteers; they're soldiers. You've exemplified your character and strong command to me on several occasions. I've chosen you and your men as my first distant detachment beyond the main body of support. Your orders are to build a fortification and search for the enemy. I'm also adding a few regulars to your command."

"Yes, sir," replied Major Cooper.

"Get your men ready. Remember, if you get into a scrape, sir, fortify and hold your position until we return from Tampa Bay. I don't want to abandon the entire cove without leaving a detachment behind. I'm counting on you, Major. You'll be relieved in a few days."

More than three hundred men broke away from the column. They stood on the bluff overlooking the small lake and waited for the baggage train to pass. The main body left behind five-days worth of rations: salt pork, flour, a few cattle, and a six-pounder --just in case.

"Sir, this is the most beautiful lake I've ever seen," Captain Seymour said.

"It looks mighty refreshin'," said another.

"It sure is nice to drink good water after marchin' through swamp."

The militiamen filled their metal cups and canteens at the spring, which bubbled fine white sand out of its way.

"I bet there is good fishin' in there," a young militiaman commented when he heard a fish jump.

"We're not on leave gentlemen," Major Cooper said. He looked over the entire lake from where he stood. "We've got a lot of work to do. This bluff will give us an advantage to look out for the enemy. We'll build right here. Start cutting down pines for pickets," he ordered. Later that evening, the men sat around campfires on the bluff and cooked their last ration of Georgia bacon.

The next morning sunlight filtered through the lacy branches, and the men continued their work on the picket.

***

"Pop can we go to our secret spot after chores?" Johnny asked. Fishing was not on his mind. Instead, it was Major Mark Anthony Cooper and the Georgia militia.

As soon as they got to the lake, Pop cast out his line and slowly reeled it in to shore. The lure shimmered in the sunlight, and Johnny watched it flicker among the reeds. He saw something out of the corner of his eye. A turtle was dropping soft, round white eggs into a hole she had dug. He watched her until she covered them up and went back in the crystal clear lake.

"May I go over to the bluff?" He asked. "Maybe the fishing is better over there."

"Sure, son, be careful," Pop said.

He carried his cane pole but he was not going to the bluff side to fish. He wanted to find more clues as to what happened over there. By now, he knew his way blindfolded as he walked the narrow path around the lake. His canteen was draped over his shoulder. He stopped by the spring to fill it up. He knelt down to submerge his canteen near the mouth of the spring. When he did, the air felt cooler and the light had changed. He noticed other footprints in the sand, and knew he was not alone. He rubbed his hand along the bark of the 'landmark' tree and felt for the cannonball scar... There was nothing there! The bulged bark was gone!

"Waaaoooop!" Wails echoed across the lake.

"That sound! Seminoles!" Johnny said out loud. The hair stood up on his arms, and chills went down his spine. A rifle ball zinged past him. He grabbed his canteen and ran back up to the bluff.

"Hurry inside the picket youn' feller. 'Course it ain't quite finished. Still have more pickets to cut and post holes to dig," a southerner spoke. "Those dang Indians are shooting at us the whole time."

"Ya' is tryin to get yo'self kill't?" Another militiaman asked, scolding Johnny.

"No sir!" He replied. "How long have you been here?"

"We've been here 'bout four days. I've been on guard duty outside the picket," the Georgia man answered. "The major sends a daily guard out to scout around the fort."

"Ya' look a might small to be in the militia. Ain't you a little youn' to enlist?" Said another.

"Are you looking for Indians, too?" A volunteer asked.

"Osceola's out there. I'm sure I recognized his white plume," a man declared.

"Osceola?" Johnny perked up when he heard the chief's name. *Pop was right,* he thought.

"We know they're out there; we just can't see 'em," a volunteer said.

"Yes, sir, they keep themselves purty well hid," another soldier commented.

"Where did ya' come from?" another man asked. "I don't remember 'em marching with us."

"The milk ain't even dried on his tongue yet," a volunteer jeered.

"Stop teasin' the lad," Major Cooper defended. "What's your name son?"

Johnny looked up at the slender man, whose posture was tall and upright even in the heat.

"Let me introduce myself. Major Mark Anthony Cooper,

commander of the first Georgia Battalion."

"Major Cooper!" Johnny shook the firm hand extended to him. "You're not a ghost. Your hand is…real."

"Excuse me. I didn't catch your name young man." Major Cooper leaned forward to hear better.

He cleared his throat. "Johnny. My name is Johnny."

The major shook his hand firmly. Pop had told him he could always tell the quality of a man's character by his handshake. He never understood what that meant until now.

"My youngest son's name is John. He is about two years old, but I bet he'll grow up to be a fine young soldier, just like you." The major smiled. "How old are you?"

"Ten, sir." Johnny's mouth suddenly felt very dry. He could not speak. He took a sip of water and closed his eyes for a second; then opened them again.

Nope, he's still here, he thought.

"My oldest daughter, Volumanie, is about your age. Do you have any brothers and sisters?"

"No, sir," Johnny replied.

"I said goodbye to two daughters and two sons in January to come to Florida. We've been marching with the right wing under the command of General Scott. He detached us the first of April."

"April? But this is…" Johnny interjected.

A militiaman interrupted. "You must be one of the settlers we came to protect. You folks had any trouble with savages?"

"No, sir."

"Sir, there is cattle across the lake," a regular reported to the major.

"Is that your cattle, son?" The major asked.

"No, sir."

"The Indians must've brought them to the lake for water and discovered we were here," a volunteer suggested.

"There looks to be a few hundred, sir," a soldier reported.

"Best you stay in the picket, son. No tellin' what might happen if you go home now," the major advised.

"Do you miss them, sir? Your children?" Johnny asked.

"Yes, I miss them, but I came here to serve my country. That's what a good soldier does. I felt it was my duty to help set things right. God always calls us to serve him and challenges us with the task at hand. I prayed, 'Lord 'let thy will be done,' and General Scott detached us here on this bluff overlooking this shining lake."

"It is called Lake Holathlikaha," Johnny said. "It means shiny or grassy--maybe both."

"Where did your folks settle? Do you have a farm close by?" a volunteer asked.

"Yes, sir," Johnny said, smiling. "You are standing on some of it."

"Get outside the picket and fire your muskets. Some Indians advanced!" A captain shouted.

In the woods behind them, another group of men chopped down pine trees. Johnny heard the trees hit the ground. When he turned around, he saw the back wall was unfinished. The men shaved one end of the logs to a point, like giant pencils. They carried them over and stuck them into deep holes, standing them upright and close together to form a picket wall.

Major Cooper gave the order. "Get the cannon ready. Fire!"

Johnny stuck his fingers in his ears when he saw the men ignite the cord.

Ka-boom.

A thunderous six-pounder sailed through the air and grazed an oak tree. His eyes widened as he witnessed the landmark tree hit in the crossfire. Major Cooper continued to send companies of men out of the picket to sally forth in pursuit of the enemy. The Seminoles came and went as they pleased, while Major Cooper's men persisted in building their defense.

"We just completed our blockhouse for the six-pounder, but we're still fortifying the rear," Major Cooper said. "We're out of rations. We ate the last of our bacon the other day, and General Scott said it would be about five days until the relief troops return."

Johnny asked, "Do you think it's safe for me to leave, sir?"

"The Hancock Blues are on guard today. Captain Brown, can you have some of your men escort this young soldier back to his home? I cannot, in good conscience, send him out in the woods alone with Indians roaming free." Major Cooper smiled.

"It was really nice to meet you, Major," Johnny saluted him. "Sir, did you notice your six-pounder hit the oak tree?"

"I did, my young friend."

"Do you think it scared the Indians?" Johnny asked. "Are you afraid?"

"A man is steadfast in the Lord's word and strong in his faith when he becomes like this tree planted near water. Jeremiah seventeen, verse seven. Do you know the verse? *Blessed is the man that trusteth the Lord, and whose hope the Lord is. For he shall be as a tree planted by the waters and that spreadeth out her roots by the river. It shall not see when heat cometh, but her leaf shall be green and shall not be careful in the year of drought, neither shall cease from yielding fruit.*" After Major Cooper recited the scripture verse, he extended his hand. "Godspeed, my friend."

"Godspeed," Johnny repeated as they shook farewell.

The militiamen guarded Johnny as they walked through the scrub palmetto.

"Aren't you afraid of Osceola and his warriors?"

"Truthfully, I'm more afraid of gators," answered one of the militia. "At night, I lie awake and hear their deep, booming calls. We're safe as long as we stay behind that picket--from gators and Indians, that is. But mosquitoes...there is no relief from 'em."

"How about snakes?"

"Oh, they come into our bed rolls. Gotta check for the poisonous ones." The militiaman asked, "What kind of farm does your pa have?"

"Citrus; we grow citrus," Johnny answered.

"I left a small farm. Never thought I'd miss red earth. I don't understand how anything grows in this sand," the militiaman said.

"Citrus does. It grows well," Johnny said proudly.

A shot zinged through the woods, speeding by, and grazed Johnny's leg.

"Are you okay boy?"

"It was nothing. They shootin' at us?" Johnny's heart pounded. His leg burned, but he did not cry. He could not.

The militiaman pulled a cartridge out of his pocket and wrapped a musket ball and black powder inside the paper. After about thirty seconds, he pulled the string with his teeth and rammed it down the barrel with a rod. Then he pulled the trigger of his .50 caliber rifle. The flint sparked, firing the rod and the musket ball out of the barrel. He fired back at the Seminoles three times in one minute.

Johnny smelled the powder after the smoke remained. It was the same odor he had smelled after the battles along the river. They waited until things were quiet. He sat crouched behind a palmetto; afraid to stand up.

"I think it's clear now, son," the militiaman said. "Are you sure you're okay?"

"Yes, it's just a scratch. Thank you. I've never been shot at before," Johnny said.

They stopped at the edge of the clearing. He did not know how he would explain the automobile. "I can make it the rest of the way."

He turned around and waved goodbye, but the man was gone. He noticed a white plume flickering behind a tree. Johnny stopped in his tracks, and a trickle of blood ran down his leg. His heart raced when Osceola stepped out from behind the tree. Johnny did not know whether to run or stay. The great chief wore a sky-blue soldier's jacket, and his head was wrapped in a turban decorated with a white plume. His reddish brown skin was dark and leathered by the sun. His lips turned up slightly into a smile when Johnny stared into his dark striking eyes. Johnny was not sure why, but he held out his hand toward the handsome war chief. Osceola shook his hand with a firm grip, and they stared at each other for a long time. Neither of them spoke. Johnny understood the Seminole Chief wanted to stay here and so did he. They shared a common bond; a love for this place. Then, the ghost warrior disappeared like he had always done during battle. Johnny could hear Pop calling him, so he limped back on the narrow path.

"What happened to you, son?" Pop asked.

"It's nothing," he whispered. "Just a scratch from a branch…"

"We better get you home and clean your wound."

Later that night, Johnny lay in his soft bed, thinking about the militiamen sleeping on the hard ground beneath the stars. If neither wild animals nor Seminoles kept them awake, he was sure their empty stomachs would.

All summer long, he had waited to name his calf. He leaped out of bed and cried, "Major!" He could hardly wait until morning to tell Pop the calf's name and call Major to the gate.

MURIEL TUTTLE EDEN-PAUL

Chapter 20

Osceola, Seminole Chief, inspired his people to build another village out of post and palmetto fronds every time they had to move. As a young boy, he ran swift and light-footed, which aided him as a grown man. He was not afraid of hard work as it took a lot of effort for his people to survive. Even in the event of war and revenge, he remained tenderhearted, protecting the women, children and elders of his tribe. He knew how to take care of them when farming and a stable life were no longer an option. He hid his people in secret places, just like the village in the cove, about four miles from Lake Holathlikaha. The Seminoles adapted to their new life in the swamp. They were survivors; fished in the rivers, lakes, and ponds and hunted in the woods for small game and white-tailed deer. Sometimes they even had the opportunity to plant corn in dry uplands.

A group of young Seminole men brought their cattle to drink from the clear grassy waters. They were shocked to hear hammering and strange voices. They ran swift like arrows, leaving their cattle behind, back to their village. Osceola's wife, Morning Star, was mixing coontie flour and honey-water in brushed pottery. She looked up at the men, "What's the matter?" She understood the look on their faces. "There are more aren't there?"

"We have to talk to Osceola," they said.

Osceola walked over to them with a spear full of largemouth bass he had caught for their supper. "What is it?"

"The white men are on the other side of the Holathlikaha. We saw Clinch's oxen and cattle. They're chopping down trees and hammering."

"Are they stacking logs?" Osceola asked, as he had seen them do many times building a breastwork.

"No, they're standing them straight up," they answered.

Osceola looked stern. "That only means one thing; the white men are staying."

Osceola had wanted to live in peace with the white man, but betrayal and revenge turned him bitter after his experience with the great council and lies of the 'white father'. Once again, he would protect his homeland and his family because he understood red men and white men could not live together in peace.

The Seminoles returned to the bluff where the cattle and oxen grazed and took them back to their village. In the evening, they hid behind tall grasses and shrub along the shore of Lake Holathlikaha.

"We want Clinch," they yelled. "Clinch, come out and fight!"

Major Cooper and his men heard the voices call out. The darkness carried the message inside their picket.

"You killed our men. We want a fair fight," the Seminoles yelled. "We're fighting for our hunting grounds."

"Come out to us and fight. Do you have rum?" another warrior yelled out into the night.

"Because we have Clinch's cattle, they must think he's here." Major Cooper suggested. "Commence firing on them."

The Georgia battalion answered the Seminoles with gunfire, firing into the darkness until the Seminoles ran off.

On the fourth day, Seminoles returned by the hundreds. Osceola had rounded up several hundred warriors to attack the picket. The Seminoles attacked from behind trees and then fell to the ground to reload and fire again. The warriors advanced from tree to tree until they were a few yards from the fort.

Major Cooper ordered, "Captain Seymour, take about seventy-five of your men and guard the exterior. Fight and drive away the enemy so the others can keep working on the picket. We must keep the fighting outside of the fort walls at all times."

"Yes, sir."

This was a daily occurrence. One day in particular, while some of the militia axed down small longleaf yellow pine and laurel oaks for the back wall, warriors besieged the fort. The Morgan Guard advanced behind trees, firing at the Seminoles. Private Zaddock Cook left the protection of the woods and planted himself out in the open.

"Cook, what are you doin'? Take cover!" The men shouted.

Captain Foster yelled, "Private git yo'self undercover, *now.*"

A whizzing bullet struck him, and he died within minutes. Since they were under fire, they had to leave his body out in the open where he lay. A few Seminoles were killed also, but their red brothers instantly carried them off as soon as their bodies hit the ground. They feared more of the dead being scalped than being killed themselves.

For thirteen consecutive days, they had one man killed, twenty wounded, and no sign of General Clinch. Major Cooper, the Georgia militia, and a few regulars ate their rations for that day, but it was not enough to fill the belly of a man. They slept at night in the safety of the picket and listened to the sounds of crickets and spring peepers. An owl hooted in a yellow pine tree, and bullfrogs croaked from the shore of the lake, *jug-o-rum, jug-o-rum.* That night, the bluff was peaceful, but they knew the next day would bring another attack from the Seminoles. They followed orders: hold down the fort and scrimmage with the Seminoles until help could arrive.

The next morning, Major Cooper ordered his men to stand in formation as he inspected his troops. "Men, you're good soldiers. The Indians have attacked us with great force. We've sustained the loss of one man. I don't want to lose any more. You've willingly rationed your food and your ammunition, even when it meant hand-to-hand combat to conserve your powder."

Suddenly, out of the morning mist, Osceola's shrill war whoop echoed across the lake. "Yo-ho-e-hee!" His yelp made the blood of his enemies chill to the bone yet it inspired his comrades. They too, ensued with more shouts and yells. The tranquil morning was disrupted with gunfire from behind longleaf pine and palmettos. It seemed no different than any other day. The Georgia militia bravely sought out the enemy and pursued them into the woods around Lake Holathlikaha. Spiral-bore, grooved rifles and muskets exchanged fire; after seconds of reloading, shots were fired again. The six-pounder cannon did not frighten off the brave warriors who watched the cannonballs sail over their heads.

Osceola was determined to keep his word, *We will fight until our last drop of blood falls on our hunting grounds, and death for our enemy.*

Several days later, April eighteenth, General Clinch encamped four miles from Fort Cooper and sent a guide and a guard to locate Major Cooper and the Georgia militia.

"We've been gone longer than we told the major," Clinch stated. "Captain Malone, detach two companies of mounted men from Jefferson and Washington Counties. Also, take some wagons and provisions to relieve Major Cooper of his duty. Give him these orders: he is to return to the main body."

The men traveled about three miles toward Fort Cooper. Once again, the Seminoles set up an ambush and opened fire on the men. They took their position in the piney woods and fired back. It was uncertain why the red men retreated, but they did. Captain Malone's priority was to get to Major Cooper, so he continued in that direction. Inside the finished frontier fort, the gaunt militia had waited sixteen days until relief arrived. Major Cooper's strong faith kept him confident help would come.

He hummed quietly a song of Zion. *Children called to Christ, how sweet the flowerets in April and May! But often the frost makes them wither away. Like flowers you may fade. Are you ready to die? While yet there is room, to a Savior fly.* Then he prayed, "Dear Father in Heaven, I've followed orders and served my country. The Indians stole our few cattle. Our provisions have been used up, and we still have some ammunition. The men are weak, but they continue, as soldiers should. In times of trouble, of joy, or darkness," Major Cooper continued, *'Cast thy burden upon thee Lord, and he shall sustain thee. He shall never suffer the righteous to be moved.'* Yes, Lord, you have sustained my men and me. Amen."

On the eighteenth day, noises from harnesses rattled and wagon wheels creaked through the palmettos. These were the sounds the men waited for.

"They're here. The relief troops are here. They've come for us." The men cheered and raised their arms, hailing the approaching guard. Major Cooper, the gallant and brave commander, left the fort to greet him.

"Major Cooper, we've brought rations for your men and orders for you to return to the main body. General Clinch is waiting four miles away," Captain Malone said.

"We're much obliged," Major Cooper said.

"We ran into some enemy fire on the way here. Have you had any action?" the captain asked.

"Daily," the major stated. "We've fought the enemy outside the picket. We advanced towards them and met with heavy fire. Sometimes the fighting lasted a few hours each day. Sometimes we fired upon them at night, even then, they came back the next day."

"If you don't mind me saying, sir," a lieutenant said, "We've all hoped to experience what you and your men have. This campaign has been a disappointment for most of us."

"How many Indians did you get, sir?" Captain Malone asked.

"I'm not sure. As soon as one of theirs fell, they quickly carried him off," Major Cooper replied.

"You carried out your duties bravely, sir," Captain Malone

commended.

The militiamen saluted their commander and left Lake Holathlikaha.

Major Cooper took one last look at the picket, which stood on the bluff. He looked over the pristine clear lake. "This was the most beautiful place I've seen since we started this campaign. I will have to return in peaceful times and bring my fishing pole." Major Cooper remarked. Propped against the scarred oak tree was a cane pole. "By the way, Captain, did you notice any citrus farms nearby?"

"No sir, there are not any homesteads along here," Captain replied.

"Hmm?" Major Cooper stroked his chin, "Curious, very curious indeed."

They marched on the military road back to Fort Brooke and then to Georgia. Major Cooper, the Georgia militia, and a few soldiers returned to their tour of duty or red clay farms. Fort Cooper served as an observation and dispatch post through 1842 when the Seminole War campaign ended.

Chapter 21

Forty-eight years after the abandonment of Fort Cooper, William J. Nelson traveled the backwoods of Hernando County to a town named after General Edmund P. Gaines--Gainesville. Mr. Nelson tied his thin mare to a hitching post on the dusty street. Her straggly bangs hung in her eyes while she chewed the metal bit in her mouth. Nelson wore a gray coat and tall black leather boots. There was a white sign nailed above the door, which read, *Land Grant Office*. His footsteps creaked on the planked walkway into the clapboard building.

Once inside, he found Mr. Benjamin Harris seated behind his large square desk stacked with papers, bound maps, and an inkwell. Harris's thin hair was plastered to his skin with salve and tonic water. His fingers were stained with black ink and yellow tobacco. "Mr. Nelson, I've been expectin' you. I got your post. How's your ride?"

"Mr. Harris." The men shook hands. "It was a pleasant ride. I stayed in the boardin' house down the street. Thank you kindly for meetin' me this mornin'. I want to make it back home by dark."

"Yes, sir, shouldn't be a problem. I've got your paperwork started right here. Have a seat." Mr. Harris gestured to the wooden chair in front of him.

He dipped his pen in the ink and wrote in his finest script, *William J Nelson of Hernando County, Florida.* Then he read aloud, *"Has deposited in the General Land Office of the United States a Certificate of the Register of the Land Office at..."* He dipped his pen again and wrote, *Gainesville, Florida,* and then he read, *"Whereby it appears that full payment has been made by the said William J Nelso*n--that would be you, sir."

The black ink scripted a flowing curly line, then down, up, down, and out again to form the "W". He artistically formed each letter spelling out Mr. Nelson's name.

Mr. Harris continued to read the document. *"According to the provisions of the Act of Congress of the twenty-fourth of April, 1820, entitled 'An Act of making further provision for the sale of the Public Lands' and the acts supplemental thereto, for..."* Then he wrote out the legal description of land describing the parcel known to be east of the *'Tallahassee Meridian in Florida containing one hundred and fifty-nine acres and ninety-nine hundredth of an acre'* in accordance with the surveyors official plat. This description described the parcel of land just west of the western wall of Fort Cooper, which had since been burned to the ground and not visible by the time Mr. Nelson became the new owner on April twenty-eighth, 1890.

"Congratulations Mr. Nelson, she's all yours!" He handed Mr. Nelson the papers.

"Thank you kindly, sir." Mr. Nelson folded the papers neatly in his leather envelope, tucked them into his saddlebag, and headed for home. Newly married and head of his household, he and his bride were officially homesteaders. If he could make a living off the land for five years, it was his.

Meanwhile, Mrs. Nelson finished loading the wagon with a mattress, pots and pans, a few bundles of clothing, and several yards of fabric. For a wedding gift, her mother had given her something she remembered as a child--a small statue of a Parian horse that once sat upon the mantle in their North Carolina cabin. She carefully wrapped it in layers of fabric and set it in the trunk for safekeeping. Her bonnet had fallen behind her neck, exposing wispy brown strands on her forehead. The hem of her faded, dainty, blue flora calico dress fell to her ankles. She tied a plain white apron around her thin waist and then sat on the step to lace up her black boots for her journey. She looked up when she heard her handsome new husband ride toward her. He patted his saddlebag and smiled. She knew everything had gone well at the Land Grant Office.

He climbed off his horse and kissed her forehead before adjusting her bonnet. With his hands around her waist, he lifted her up and twirled her.

"Mr. Nelson!" She giggled.

The leather envelope was opened and he waved the document above her head.

"Our new place! We leave at dawn. I'm ready to work hard and make a living off our land."

"Me too," she smiled.

They were newcomers to the area and wanted to take advantage of the government's land grant program. Almost one hundred sixty acres, *one hundred and fifty-nine acres and ninety-nine hundredth of an acre*, to be exact, the Nelsons' property sat in the interior of the cove area. The next morning, they traveled miles of soft, sandy roads used by the military during the Second Seminole War. They followed the road through sandy uplands of pinewoods and acres of dense palmetto clumps. Mrs. Nelson drew in a deep breath of the late April air. It was clear and clean, just like the beautiful shiny lake before her.

"Mr. Nelson," she said with delight, "that's probably the most picturesque lake I've ever seen."

He lifted his wife out of the wagon, unharnessed the mare, and untied their scrawny cow. They walked the cow and the mare to the spring where they drank from the gentle burble. The cowbell clanked as she wandered off to eat some grass. The mare followed her and whinnied with pleasure to be out of her harness.

Mrs. Nelson took off her bonnet and laid it in her lap. She saw her face reflected in the glistening water. "Oh my!" She exclaimed, "I do look a mess, Mr. Nelson."

She scooped the clear water in her hands and splashed it on her face. She pulled out a bright, blue handkerchief and gently pat-dried her skin. Then she cupped her hands to drink. "Delicious! Its so refreshing!" she exclaimed.

Mr. Nelson knelt down beside her. "I think you look beautiful, Mrs. Nelson," he said, and he kissed her on the cheek. He also scooped water and drank. "Mighty fine, Mrs. Nelson, mighty fine. We're truly blessed."

"Do we have neighbors?" she asked feeling the isolation.

"I know there is a church in Istachatta about ten miles away. We can visit sometime and meet the neighbors," he assured her. "Right now, we've plenty of pine and oak to build our cabin."

She smiled, "I'm hungry; are you?"

She went to the wagon and brought out some bread and salted venison wrapped in red gingham, which she had prepared earlier.

"I wonder what happened here?" Mr. Nelson rubbed his hand across the bulge of an oak tree. "Looks like something heavy hit it".

They sat beneath the sprawling branches of the Landmark tree.

"I do recall Mr. Harris sayin' Indians lived in the cove, and battles were fought around here."

"Indians around here?" She asked alarmed. She stop loosening the string, which tied the gingham bundled.

"No, not anymore. They sent them out west and down south is my understandin'. This is a good place," he said proudly. "We won't starve here, that's fo' sure. We can catch fish, frogs, and turtles in the lake, and there's plenty of deer."

"It's beautiful here. There's a fine place for a garden. I brought bean, corn, and squash seeds. We can grow lots of sweet potato. I can pick wild berries, grapes, and…there are always acorns. I'd like our cabin just west. There--," she pointed. "If that's alright with you." She took a deep breath and wrapped her arms around her husband. "I'm so thankful for all God's provisions."

"After we build our cabin, I'll start buying cattle and hogs. This is going to be good grazin' land. They'll have plenty of fresh water to drink. I can sell cattle about five dollars a head. I just need to round them up at market time." He smiled and held his wife. They were confident that they would make it in this place.

They spent their first night sleeping in their wagon, under the same stars as the militia and Seminoles, dreaming about tomorrow as homesteaders.

Chapter 22

More than one hundred years later, after Major Cooper and his men left the shores of lake Holathlikaha, the excavation of the picket was underway. Johnny pulled his red truck in front of Live Oak Manor, Mr. Emil was waiting at the front door in his wheel chair.

"He's been up since the crack of dawn," the nurse greeted.

"Good morning Johnny," welcomed Mr. Emil. "I could hardly sleep last night after you called me."

"I've got a lot of people for you to meet." Johnny wheeled Mr. Emil out to his truck and helped him into the cab. Then he put the wheelchair in the back. "Betty'll meet us out there." As they drove to the fort site, Johnny filled in Mr. Emil on the details. He parked the truck as close as he could get to the bluff area.

Mr. Emil surprised, said, "Look at all these cars! Who all's out here?"

"The archeology team and newspaper reporters," Johnny wheeled the chair close to Mr. Emil. "Hop on Partner!"

Johnny introduced Mr. Emil to the team. "This gentlemen showed me the landmark tree and shared the oral history when I came to Florida my first summer."

"It sure's good to meet you," said Professor Frank. "If it had not been for you; we might not be standing here today!"

The thin wheels of the chair stuck in the soft sand. "Oh, this is too much trouble, son," Mr. Emil felt frustrated. "These ol' legs just don't work like they used to. Just leave me right here."

Professor Frank jumped over. "Here, let me help. We'll get you there; don't you worry about that."

"When Johnny was a boy, we would come out here fishin'. Did he ever tell you about the biggest bass ever caught in the county?" Mr. Emil asked. He caught it right here in Lake Holathlikaha."

"Oh, I think my record has been beat since then," Johnny laughed.

Mr. Emil was saddened to see the bluff torn up. "Oh my, this doesn't look like what I remember. I don't know what to look at first. The mounds of dirt, equipment, and… your bulldozer!"

"Yes, sir, and he did a fine job with it," the professor defended.

"It don't surprise me none. Once, he dug out our courthouse basement with his Ford Ferguson," Mr. Emil chuckled.

"Don't worry, Mr. Emil. Everything will be put back when we're done," Johnny assured him.

"That's right. You'll never know we were here," Professor Frank added.

"What happened to the landmark tree? Did you cut it down?" Mr. Emil asked sadly.

"No, a hurricane brought it down few years back," Johnny reminded him.

"That's right; you told me."

"Hey, Mr. Emil." Betty and Abby gave him a hug.

"Here, let's get you closer to the trenches. We've found the perimeter of the fort." Johnny pushed the wheelchair closer.

Mr. Emil peered into the trench. "Would you look at that! Land sakes. It's right where we thought it was. Can't you just see Major Cooper standin' here sayin', 'This bluff will give us an advantage to look out for the enemy'?"

"He ordered the men to cut the pine and build the picket right here," Johnny stated.

"Yes, each one of those circles of dark soil is a post mold, which indicates the perimeter of Fort Cooper," explained Professor Frank. "It covers almost an acre of land."

"Well, I'll be! That's a lot of picket to cut while under Indian fire," Mr. Emil said.

"Yes," the professor agreed, "and you can tell because the pickets are set in a zigzag pattern, and the sizes vary. They shoveled the trench, sharpened each end of the picket, and set them into the ground. Often, they chinked in another piece of wood for stability. They were in a hurry to get the job done, but we've proof they finished and did so under the attack of the enemy."

"Mr. Emil, look at all the 'tifacts we found," said Abby. "I helped find this...a musket ball."

"We also found hand-forged nails and a jacket button." Johnny showed Mr. Emil, "Here's a metal cup."

"Just think; a militiaman drank spring water out of this cup," Mr. Emil said. "Now Abby, which do you think would taste better, coffee made from swamp water or clear spring water?"

She giggled.

"Here are some arrowheads which pre-date the Seminoles," Professor Frank held them in his hand. "Clearly, our excavation designates this land a historic site. It's a rare find. It's the only Seminole War fort site, which has been left undisturbed. This is the only fort from the entire Seminole War that will be available to the public. Fort Drane, Fort King, and Fort Brooke were significant forts during that time. Fort Brooke has been lost forever, buried beneath Tampa."

Johnny said thoughtfully, "I wish Pop was here to see this. We've put an 'X' back on the map."

"He knows. He knows," assured Mr. Emil.

Chapter 23

Fort Cooper State Park had been opened for about ten years. Johnny penciled in the third weekend in March, *Fort Cooper Days.*

"Betty, where are they?" Johnny asked as he looked at his watch. "They should've been here hours ago."

"You'll get there in plenty of time." She kissed him on the cheek, "Look, here they come now!"

"Hey, Daddy. I'm sorry I'm late. I overslept." His daughter apologized. "Mama, you ready for our girl's day out? You have fun, Spencer, and mind your granddaddy!"

"See ya later, alligator!" Spencer called to them as they drove down the lane.

Johnny tousled his grandson's golden hair and said, "Ready?"

"Yes, sir." They climbed into his old red Ford truck and headed down the lane.

"You see those trees? The big ones?"

"Yes, sir."

"I helped my Pop, your great-granddaddy, plant those when I was just about your age. And see those young trees there?" Johnny pointed. "Tangerines. Your mama helped me plant those."

The truck came to a stop. "Jump out, open and close the gate for me. We're going in the back way. I've got my own shortcut."

He smiled. Spencer opened the heavy truck door that creaked. *Thud!* He slammed it hard.

"Hey, partner, don't slam my door!"

Spencer unlatched the chains from the gate, and when his Granddaddy passed through, he hooked them back again.

"Granddaddy, can I ride on the tailgate, please?"

"Sure," Johnny waited for Spencer to lower the tailgate and climb aboard.

Spencer banged the bed of the truck to let Johnny know he was ready. He hung his feet down as they bounced over the bumps, and sometimes touched the ground. He'd heard stories how his mother, her sisters, and brother would ride through the pasture where Brahmas and Black Angus grazed to get to the other side.

It was a beautiful spring morning. The park ranger waved them on. Granddaddy stopped and said, "Two please."

"You know you don't have to pay," the ranger answered.

"It's a good cause," Johnny insisted. "Lot of people coming through yet?"

"Quite a few!"

Spencer banged on the truck bed and teased, "Granddaddy there're people behind us. You're holdin' up traffic!"

"I guess I am. See you later."

Johnny parked his truck in the lot under the shade of an oak tree. "The lake looks pretty today, clear and sparkling."

"Can I go swimmin' later?" Spencer asked.

"Sure, why not? Did I ever tell you the time I caught the biggest bass in the lake?" Granddaddy asked.

Spencer had heard the story, but he didn't mind hearing it again.

"It was so big, I was scared I would lose it. It took your great-granddaddy, your great-great-granddaddy, and Mr. Emil to help me pull it in."

"What did you do with it?" Spencer asked.

"We cooked it and ate it that night for supper," Johnny chuckled.

"Besides, we had to eat the evidence. We didn't want to give our secret fishing spot away."

"Boy, something sure smells good," Spencer said as he breathed in deep smoky-woodsy air.

"Somebody must be cooking up some good vittles," Johnny pointed. "There is someone... Looks like a Seminole."

"Would you like to try to sofkee?" The woman offered.

Spencer asked, "What's in it?"

"It's made with rice."

"No, thank you," he said politely. "What's cooking in your pot?"

"Acorn stew. I'm waiting for our men to come back. They'll need food after their battle."

"I hope they come back soon. It sure smells good," Spencer said. "Goodbye".

"We need to get to the bluff. Listen to that red cardinal overhead; he's telling us to hurry up," Johnny encouraged.

The trail was flanked with saw palmettos. The sun's rays had not yet reached the hammock floor, so fronds were still wet with morning dew. A yellow butterfly fluttered between wood violets, then flit its wings to a cluster of little white flowers. They found a nice spot to sit so they could see everything. In about ten minutes, it would start.

Johnny shook hands with some people from town, but Spencer was not interested in their conversation. He was more interested in the wood hammock. A feathered plume flickered behind a tree; there was movement in the saw palmettos. A gun barrel poked around a tree and then disappeared. He heard a horse whinny in the distance. Men in uniform were gathered around pine trees, sharpening them with an ax, like a giant pencil.

Suddenly, without warning, came cries of, "Ya-Hoooop! Eeeeee-Yah!"

The sounds of gunfire disturbed the silence of the shore of Lake Holathlikaha once again. The Georgia militia fired their spiral-bore, grooved rifles, while others behind them continued to build the picket walls under enemy gunfire. The Seminoles fired their muskets, and arrows toward the militia. Two men loaded the barrel of a six-pounder.

"Fire!" shouted the captain. The huge explosion from the cannon's blast rumbled across the lake like thunder. Smoke from the blast lingered close to low hanging moss.

The ghost warriors fought bravely and fearlessly; the cannon did not hinder their advancement. Soon Seminoles came out of hiding. Their faces were painted for battle--half-black and half-red, which meant 'death to their enemy.' They advanced up the bluff toward the picket and also attacked from behind.

Major Cooper ordered, "Captain Meriwether and Captain Seymour, get your men outside of the fort to fight and drive off the enemy. We have to hold our position, men!"

Visitors no longer heard birds sing, fish jump, or squirrels leap from tree to tree. Instead, men sallied, using knifes, swords, or fist. Bodies hit against one another. They rolled, punched, kicked, or thrust their knives until men retreated or lay lifeless on the ground.

It was silent again. Smoke lingered. The dead and wounded lay where they fell. Seminoles vanished into the tall reeds and escaped across the lake. They would go back to their home in the cove, where the women, children, and elders waited for them. The wounded were brought to the healer. The women fed them sofkee and acorn stew. Then they rested to fight once more, defending their homeland.

The militia continued to build their fort and hoped to get more pickets up before their next attack. They moved about the bluff with caution. Surprise attacks from the Seminoles taught them to be ready at all times.

Major Cooper sat tall in his saddle. "Men we were given orders to fortify and hold our position until General Scott returns from Tampa." He commanded his troops, "We need to ration our sustenance until relief troops arrive."

He left the scene on horseback disappearing into the woods.

"Good morning. Welcome to Fort Cooper Day," a park ranger greeted the audience. Speaking into a microphone, he brought the audience back to the twentieth century. "Look around you. The landscape you see today is the same as it was for Osceola, and his warriors, Major Cooper, and his troops. The spirits from the past came to life today to tell you the living history of what happened a century and half ago. The Friends of Fort Cooper have made this weekend possible."

Loud applause from the crowd interrupted him.

"They welcome any questions you have as you walk around your beautiful state park. Please visit the encampments and demonstration tents scattered under the hammock. If you swim in the clear, shiny waters of Lake Holathlikaha, or canoe to the opposite shore, imagine yourself a Seminole warrior fighting for his beloved Florida. As you hike the nature trails, you just might hear the creak of wagon wheels. It could be that of General Scott's relief troops. Or maybe it is settlers looking for their homestead. You never know what sights, smells, and sounds will bring to your experience. Our next reenactment will be at two this afternoon. I hope you enjoy your visit."

The audience applauded. Spencer watched as the re-enactors stood up and brushed off leaves and dirt. The men gathered their weapons and joined the rest of the troops or tribe. The audience began making their way through the park, along with Johnny and his grandson.

"Let's watch this guy," Spencer tugged Granddaddy over to a blacksmith.

The black mare waited, patiently harnessed in leather and brass. The burly, black-bearded man held iron nails between his teeth. He held up a hoof and hammered on the new horseshoe he had made.

"That looks like it hurts," Spencer said, concerned.

The horse was swishing her tail to get the flies off her back.

"She's okay; she likes the attention," the blacksmith said, going back to his work.

"I'm hot, Granddaddy. Let's get something to drink and go for a swim. Last one in is a rotten egg!"

"Wait a minute. I thought you wanted something to drink?" Granddaddy watched his grandson's energy as the boy ran toward the beach, kicked off his shoes, and splashed into the water.

"I remember those days." He said to himself as he walked to a canopy, "Two Cokes, please."

"Do you need a straw?" The lady asked.

"Yes ma'am, two. Thank you."

Johnny sat on the beach and watched his grandson swim. "Coke!" he called and raised the cup for Spencer to see.

"I'll be right there," he yelled from the water.

Later, the sun was setting, and most of people had gone home. The fires had been extinguished; the smoke looked like a fine veil attached to branches.

"It's time to go!" Johnny called out.

"One more jump, please?" Spencer begged.

Johnny held up five fingers for five more minutes. He wrapped his arms around his legs and sat on the sandy beach. The water's surface sparkled with flecks of gold, shimmering in the sun. A blue heron fished for minnows caught in thick reeds along the shore. It became quiet; the thick hammock surrounding the lake silenced even Spencer's splashes.

Johnny reflected when he was that young boy swimming in the lake. Pop had sat, as he sat now, watching him, or maybe he would throw out a cast from the shore. Johnny had been awestruck with this place since that first summer and still continued to marvel it. A mysterious allure existed; this he could not deny. It helped him to see and feel the presence of others as he shared their stories. It gave him the perseverance to search for the picket. He understood the lives of those who came before him, and felt their presence nearby.

Mr. Emil and Pop stood on either side of him and watched another generation splash in Lake Holathlikaha. At that moment, a broad hand tousled his hair. A firm hand patted his shoulder as if to say, *Job well done, my son.*

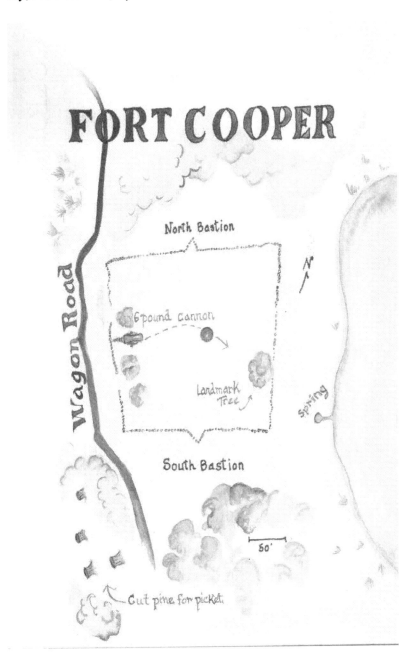

FORT COOPER

North Bastion

Wagon Road

6-pound cannon

Landmark Tree

South Bastion

Spring

N

50'

Cut pine for picket

MURIEL TUTTLE EDEN-PAUL

EPILOGUE

Four years after the first excavation, another team returned to the fort site, and archeologist Henry Baker conducted the dig. Unfortunately, the trenches from the first excavation had not been backfilled as promised to Mr. Emil. The ghostly picket remains were washed by rain, and motorcyclists vandalized the trenches. This valuable trace of the past, where the picket once stood, had been nothing more than a racetrack to them. The intention of the second excavation was to find the blockhouse, which Major Cooper had described in his journals. There was speculation it was situated by the west wall, due to a heavy saturation of nails and charred clay discovered in that area. The exact location of the blockhouse still remained a mystery; as did the remains of the only known fatality, Coronet Zaddock Cook of the Georgia Battalion, Morgan Guard Company.

The fort remained an outpost for dispatch and observation through the end of the Second Seminole War. Afterward, this "X" slowly faded off the map and was forgotten just like the others. The picket had burned to the ground, leaving only the burned post molds buried beneath layers of sand and debris.

Archeologist Baker and his team surveyed an area west of the fort site and discovered limestone rocks set in a "U" shape. It was thought to be a pioneer hearth for cooking, but there was no confirmation of a cook fire. There was evidence, however, which uncovered a pioneer's trash pit, which homesteaders had left behind. Perhaps, a young couple who could not endure the harsh life in the piney backwoods. Fragments of settlers' lives were unearthed and preserved--the heel of a woman's shoe and a Parian headless horse statue, as well as other items, were found. A land grant made out to William J. Nelson does exist, but no one knew what happened after that.

The following two years continued with funding, field research, and Johnny's personal efforts and dedication. Since that little boy spent his first summer with Pop; discovering Fort Cooper became true. The fruition of his life-long dream became Fort Cooper State Park, when it officially opened in 1977.

When Major Cooper returned to his home in Georgia, he was awarded a hero's welcome. He lived his life as a husband, father, citizen soldier, lawyer, banker, faithful servant of God, educator, farmer, founder of iron works, and politician.

Chief Osceola lived his life as husband, father, orator, warrior, military strategist, defender of Florida, and advocate for the Seminole people. When he was captured under a white flag, he spoke of peace for his people to live in south Florida. He took off his turban, removed the plume, and handed it to General Jessup.

"Give this to my white father to show him that Osceola will do as you have said." He was sad and heartbroken.

Upon his death in 1938, in Fort Moultrie South Carolina, the newspapers awarded this hero the 'most famous Native American'.

April is a month of meaningful coincidence. April 1836 marks the anniversary of Major Cooper and his men being relieved of their position on the bluff. April twenty-eighth 1890, a newlywed couple made their homestead there. April seventh, 1891, was Pop's birthday, the man who introduced his son, Johnny, to the maps marked with "X's" and the river, which took him there. April seventh, 2010, the family and community celebrated Johnny's life as a husband, father, sailor, citrus farmer, historian, environmentalist, and faithful preserver of the past, upon the bluff overlooking Lake Holathlikaha. Betty, their daughters, and son prepared the celebration. They found Pop's old wooden nail barrels in the rafters of the red pole barn and filled them with white roses, stratus altroneia, baby's breath, and spireia. They gathered fragile wisteria flowers from the piney woods, tucking them gently into the barrels along with fresh cut orange blossoms. Then it was time for them to take the road through the woods and palmetto fronds to the bluff. During the ceremony, Johnny's grandchildren tossed white and lavender blossoms, which were carried by a gentle breeze and sparkled in the afternoon sun. It was a perfect day.

In April, one hundred and seventy-four years later, all who gathered at this place lifted their voices and sang.

Swing low, sweet chariot, Comin' for to carry me home....

After we sang the final lines, *Tell all my friends I'm comin' too, Comin' for to carry me home.*

In between the pine trees and turkey oaks, I saw a white plume flicker in the sun's rays. The shiny brass buttons of a tall Georgian glistened in the sunlight. A trim, blond-haired man, bronzed by the Florida sun, wore tan shorts, with a white, two-pocket shirt tucked into his belt, attached with a yellow tape measure. On his feet, he wore light brown, round-toed, leather cowboy boots. His step turned slightly outwards as he walked with a purposeful gait to join the others. We honored not only one man that day, but three, who were gallant defenders of what they believed in. Osceola and Major Cooper came to carry Johnny home. He departed with them to protect these piney woods.

"Goodbye, Daddy."

AUTHOR BIOGRAPHY

Muriel T. Eden-Paul was born and raised in the cove area of the Withlacoochee River. In her lifetime, she camped on the bluff of Lake Holathlikaha before it became a state park. She, along with her brother and sisters, experienced first-hand, the archeological excavation of a historical site. Muriel now lives with her husband and children in SE Wisconsin.

BIBLIOGRAPHY

BOOKS

Barbour, George M. Florida for Tourists, Invalids, and Settlers . A
    Facsimile   Reproduction of the 1882 Edition; Quadricentennial
    Edition of the Floridiana Facsimile Reprint Series. Gainesville:
    University of Florida Press, 1964.

Bemrose, John. Edited by Mahon, John K. Reminiscences of the Second
    Seminole War.
    Gainesville: University of Florida Press, 1966.

Brooks, Barbara. The Seminole. Vero Beach: Rourke Publications, Inc.,
    1989.

Cohen, M. M.. Notices of Florida and The Campaigns, Gainesville:
    University of Florida Press, 1964. (reproduction of the 1836
    Edition)

Dunn, Hampton. Back Home . Citrus County Bicentennial Steering
    Committee, 1976.

Garbarino, Merwyn S. The Seminole. New York: Chelsea House
    Publishers, 1989.

Mahon, John. History of Second Seminole War. Gainesville: University
    Press of Florida, 1985 revised edition.

Maiken, Peter T., Night Trains., Chicago: Lakme Press, 1989

McNeer, May. War Chief of the Seminole . New York: Random House,
    1954.

Spraque, John T., Brevet Captain, Eighth Regiment, U.S. Infantry.
    Origin, Progress, and Conclusion of the Florida War. A Facsimile
    Reproduction of the 1848 Edition; Quadricentennial Edition of the
    Floridiana Facsimile Reprint Series. Gainesville: University of
    Florida Press, 1964.

Patrick, Rembert W. Aristocrat in Uniform, General Duncan L. Clinch.
    Gainesville: University of Florida Press, 1963.

Potter, Woodbourne. The War in Florida: Being an Exposition of its Causes and an Accurate History of Campaigns of Generals Clinch, Gaines and Scott. Baltimore: Lewis and Coleman, 1836.

Pope, Mark Cooper III and McKee, Donald, J. The Iron Man of Georgia . Atlanta: Graphic Publishing Company, 2000.

Porterfield, James D., Dining By Rail. New York., N.Y., 1993.

Whitney, Edison L. and Perry, Frances, M. Four American Indians A Book for Young Americans. New York, Cincinnati, Chicago: American Book Company., 1904.

NEWSPAPER AND PERIODICALS

Ballard, Rick. "Come and Relive and Only..." The Citrus County Chronicle, 16 December 1971, p.6.

Bittle, George C. "The Florida Militia's Role in the Battle of the Withlacoochee". Florida Historical Quarterly. April 1966, Volume 44 Issue 4, pp.303-311.

Board, Mark F. "Asi-Yaholo or Osceola". Florida Historical Quarterly. January 1955, Volume 33 Issue 3, pp.249-305.

Brevard, Caroline Mays. "Richard Keith Call By His Granddaughter." Florida Historical Quarterly. October 1908, Volume 1 Issue 3, pp.8-20.

"Bureau of Historic Sites and Properties", Bulletin No. 5, Division of Archives, History and Records Management,

Chamberlain, Donald L. Frontier Outpost, 1824-42, University of South Florida, 1995.

Covinton, James W. "Life at Fort Brooke 1824-1836." Florida Historical Quarterly. October 1958, Volume 36 Issue 2, pp.319-330.

Dunn, Hampton. "Fort Cooper Site Theory Confirmed." Accent of Florida. The Tampa Tribune, 30 January 1972, p. 2.

Eden, John H. Jr.. "Fort Cooper April 1836." Privately Published for:
Interpretive Services Division of Recreation and Parks Department
of Natural Resources, State of Florida, Inverness, FL. R.G.
Printing Co. 1977, pp.1-4.

Elwell, Gordon R. "The Siege of Fort Cooper: Georgians and the Second
Seminole War." Georgia Militia and National Guard Society.
Spring 1989, Volume 1 No. 2.

Fryman, Brank B. Jr., "Exploratory Excavations at Fort Cooper, Citrus
County, Florida A Preliminary Report and Statement of Expenditures",
Bureau of Historic Sites and Properties Divisions of Archives, History
and Records Management Department of State, 25, May, 1972.

Fryman, Frank B. Jr.. "Fort Cooper Site Excavated." Archives and
History News. January-February 1972, Vol.3, No. 1, pp.3-4.
Eden-Paul., p. 3

Homan, Wayne "The Town Nature Reclaimed", Florida Outdoors
Magazine, May, 1957. www.qsy.com/panasoffkee/lkpana01.html, 25
April 2006

Hunter, Jim. "Fort Cooper Re-enactment." Neighbors, Citrus County
Chronicle, 15 April 1983, p.1B.

Jones, Shelia. "Fort Cooper Park is Product of Persistence, Peruasion,
Pride." Chronicle-Press Sentinel, 21 September 1975.

Mahon, John K. "The Journal of A.B. Meek and the Second Seminole
War 1836." Florida Historical Quarterly. April 1960, Volume 38
Issue 4, pp.302-318.

Moore, Michael. "Bit if History Unearthed at Fort Site." St. Petersburg
Times, 22 September 1975.

"The QUARTERLY Periodical of the Florida Historical Society",
Volume V, Number 3, January 1927,

Roberts, Albert Hubbard. "Dade Massacre." Florida Historical Quarterly.
Pepper Printing Company, Gainesville, Florida January 1927,
Volume 5 Issue 3, pp.123-138.

Twitty, Jim. "Fort Cooper – Remains of Historical Fort Discovered Near Inverness." The Tampa Tribune, 27 November, 1971.

White, Frank L., Jr. "Journals of Lt. John Pickell 1836-1837." Florida Historical Quarterly. October 1959, Volume 38 Issue 2, pp.142-172.

WORLD WIDE WEB INTERNET SOURCES AND ARTICLES

"Camp Life in Florida; A handbook for Sportsmen and Settlers.: Chapter 19. published   by Forest and Stream Publishing Company. 1876 www.feit.usf.edu/florida/docs/s/steayct.htm

Chamberlain, Donald, Frontier Outpost 1824-1842. Online. 5 March 2006.
University of South Florida, Department of History, 1995.
<www.fcit.usf.edu>

Elderkin, James D. The Seminole War, James D. Elderkin, 4th US Infantry 1899. "Biographical Sketches and Anecdotes of a Soldier of Three Wars, as Written by Himself (Detroit: 1899), pp.16-22. Online. 6 April 2006.
<http://fcit.usf.edu/FLORIDA/docs/s/semwar02.htm.>

"Florida Development", www.flheritage.com., Online. 3 March 2006. Eden-Paul., p. 4

"Forgotten Street Scenes", www.forgotten-ny.com., Online. 28 February 2006.

"History of the Dade Battlefield". Online., 23 January 2011,. www.dadebattlefield.com

McCall, George A. Letters from the Frontiers 1868. "Seminole Wars" First Lieutenant, George A. McCall, 4th Infantry. pp.1-22. Online. 6 April 2006.
<http://fcit.usf.edu/FLORIDA>

National Portrait Gallery, Smithsonian, Osceola "Black Drink"Online. 6 April 2006
www.npg.si.edu/col/native/osceola

"Porters Making down a berth" National Museum of American History, Transportation Collection., Online., 28 February, 2006. www.americanhistory.si.edu

"Suniland Magazine" 1911-1925 Articles Online, 5 March 2006 www.fcit.usf.edu

White, John C. Jr. "American Military Strategy During the Second Seminole War. Major, United States Marine Corp Thesis, April 1995. Online. 29 April 2006
<www.globalsecurity.org>

"Withlachoochee River". Online. 4 April 2006
<www.saj.usace.army.mil/conops/apc/historic-photos/withlacoochee>

"Withlacoochee River Trails." Online. 5 April 2006.
<www.dep.state.fl.us/gwt/guide/regions/crossflorida/trails/images/withlacoochee_south>
.
http://www.glorecords.blm.gov/details/patent/default.aspx?accession=FL0640__.155&docClass=STA&sid=pakcuoyp.ugf#patentDetailsTabIndex=1

"Discovery of Phosphate in Florida." Online. 17 March 2006.
<www1.fipr.state.fl.us/phosphateprimer>

"Face painting" Online 27 January 2011.
www.nativetech.org/seminole/facepainting

PERSONAL LETTERS

Correspondence to and from John H. Eden Jr.

MAPS

Map of Florida, 1840. Florida Historical Quarterly. January 1927, Volume 5 Issue 3, Frontispiece.

"Seminole War Map." Online. 6 April 2006
<www.sonofthesouth.net/americanindians/seminole~war-map.htm>

.

www.raremaps.com

http://fcit.usf.edu/Florida/maps/1900/photos

http://taplines.net/southflorida/oldmap.jpg

FORT COOPER

www.floridastatepark.org/fortcooper/default.cfm

Fort Cooper State Park
3100 South Old Floral City Road
Inverness, Florida 34450
Phone: 352-726-0315
Fax: Contact Park for Number

Citizen Support Organization
Friends of Fort Cooper, Inc.
3100 South Old Floral City Road
Inverness, FL 34450

Made in the
USA
Columbia, SC